A CORRUPT CHRISTIAN?

Being a True Christian in Today's Counter-Christian Culture

Annette Evans

Merrell Publishing Company, LLC
Seattle, WA

Merrell Publishing Company, LLC

Copyright © 2018 Annette Evans

All rights reserved. No part of this book may be reproduced or transmitted in any form or by any means, electronic or mechanical, including photocopying, recording, or by any information storage and retrieval system, without permission in writing from the publisher.

Published by Merrell Publishing Company, LLC
701 Fifth Avenue, Suite 3520
Seattle, WA 98104

First Edition.
ISBN 978-1984924179
Printed in the United States of America.

Testimonials

SAINTSOFGOLD has helped me communicate softly, lovingly and powerfully. ~ Ruby Allen, TN

Becoming a Saint of Gold fulfills me in every way. I'm a better husband, a better father, a better friend, and a better man. I recommend **SAINTSOFGOLD** to every man who wants to be a good model to his children, family and community. ~ Noel Davis, KY

SAINTSOFGOLD has been such an inspiration for me. The training, coaching, and love I received have guided me through many challenges. The simple coursework has been invaluable.
~ Steel Johnson, WA

I was a Christian for many years, but slowly and unintentionally began to lose interest and neglected daily spiritual devotion and praise. This book helped me reexamine my relationship with God and get me back on track to applying daily truths of the Word intentionally with thanksgiving. ~ Tom Naylor, MA

If you really want to fulfill God's intention on Earth, you must aspire gold status. It doesn't matter if you're a saint of silver or bronze, this program will help your aspiration. Come join us! ~ Jerry Harris, FL

I had only to be open and willing to apply **SAINTSOFGOLD** suggestions to become utterly transformed. The results are real!
~ Stephanie Allen, WA

Disclaimer

The author and Merrell Publishing Company, LLC, emphasize this material is not offered as personal or professional advice. It is highly recommended you seek the services of a competent professional before making any decisions related to religious, psychological and interpersonal issues.

Best efforts have underscored the writing of this book, but the author and publisher make no representations or warranties of any kind and assume no liabilities of any kind with respect to the accuracy or completeness of the contents, and specifically disclaim any implied warranties of use for any particular purpose.

Neither the author nor Merrell Publishing Company, LLC, shall be held liable or responsible to any person or entity with respect to any loss or incidental or consequential damages caused, or alleged to have been caused, directly or indirectly, by the information contained in this book, or disruption caused by errors or omissions, whether such errors or omissions result from negligence, accident, or any other cause.

The material represented in this book was created to show the author's belief and personal practices as guidance for replication by the reader with the intention of instilling increased personal awareness for the purpose of improved attitudes toward situational circumstances, leading to healthier and more desirable outcomes without harm or duress to any living organism. By reading this material, the reader acknowledges and accepts all responsibility for challenges and changes that may occur, and understands that results are determined by the reader's commitment and personal actions.

Dedication

This book is dedicated to the memory of my husband, Don, who lovingly helped shape the person I have become by allowing me to explore ideas of creativity and use my abilities as a young adult, which enabled me to achieve many dreams, grow in strength and use my potential even to this day.

I also dedicate this book to my parents, George and Ruby, who taught me to believe in the one and only Sovereign true God of the universe, and that Jesus is the way, the truth and the life, and without Him, life is truly no life at all, and to the many relatives, friends, and acquaintances, church affiliations or not, who have encouraged me, critiqued, loved and cared about me, challenging me to be the unique and wonderfully created woman I am.

I am thankful for my spiritual foundation, given me by my parents to not be ashamed of the gospel of Jesus Christ. I am thankful I do not struggle with unbelief of who God is and was and is to come. I am thankful that I believe that nothing is impossible with God. This book is thereby dedicated to my Lord and Savior Jesus and the Holy Spirit who worked through me to accomplish this book with thanksgiving in my heart.

About the Author

Annette Evans has been in training for being a servant to God and a servant to others for more than 35 years. She began working at an early age, beginning by assisting her mom and dad with several younger siblings, and even began teaching Sunday school at the age of eight. She worked part time for her uncle daily in her early teenage years, developing additional skills of trustworthiness and dependability.

Annette is one of 10 children. Her father, a local pastor from a small Midwestern town in Indiana, and her mother were involved in their community. In addition to being a pastor, her father was a barber and her mother a hair dresser. Annette was taught to offer support, guidance, and encouragement, starting with six younger siblings. She grew up in a loving home where the teachings of Jesus was a constant reminder of what her aim in life should be centered around, loving and living for Jesus.

Annette's excellent people skills are what most people notice immediately. Her employment experiences vary as an administrator, academic coach and mentor, supervisor, manager, TV and radio host, and business owner. She observes and notices people with compassion and care. She believes the mandate of launching **SAINTSOFGOLD** is God given, and is stepping out in faith to make available encouragement through coaching and training to as many who will make use of her services. Her passion is people. It is her desire that everyone have a spirit of excellence in whatever they do. Her ability is in training and teaching. She wants to impact the lives of everyday people using basic skills that some may not have received while others may have forgotten about them.

Her passion has always been in qualifying others more than herself. That selflessness of helping others to believe and reach for the stars is why **SAINTSofGOLD** was founded. Annette's journey continues to unfold in helping others to believe in impossibilities becoming possibilities. Her passion will continue to unfold with **SAINTSofGOLD**.

It is truly her privilege and honor to encourage, admonish and strengthen in love and in truth. As founder, she understands people, and believes simply in age-old principles such as love, patience, encouragement and truth that help people become satisfied in the process of growth in life.

It is the vision of **SAINTSofGOLD** for all to continue to strive toward the fullest capacity of living and loving in this life.

Annette Evans
Founder, **SAINTSofGOLD**

SAINTSofGOLD4u@gmail.com
www. **SAINTSofGOLD**.com
253.517.3541

SAINTSofGOLD
P. O. Box 23575
Federal Way, WA 98093

Acknowledgements

I wish to personally thank first my Lord and Savior Jesus Christ whose death, burial and resurrection was for my sins. Thank you for choosing me and thank you for your love, support, and desire given by You to write this book.

Joe Maas, my publisher and business mentor, for the years we have shared time and enjoyable conversations about business, God and the cultural climate. Thank you for all those enriching hours!

Dr. Daniel Levine, my editor and literary guide; your insights, support, personal dedication and friendship made this project fun and exciting, and also for your patience with keeping me on track with the completion of this book.

George, Bryn, Jerome, Patricia, Kenneth, Rose, Denise, Judy, and recently deceased brother Larry, as my siblings have all been a blessing to me. Thank you for accepting Jesus. I love you dearly.

To the many nieces and nephews, aunts, uncles and cousins of which there are too many to name. You are amazing and you know God's love.

To the numerous friends and colleagues who have inspired me to dream bigger and to achieve more. Thank you so much in helping me to increase in character and integrity. To God be the glory.

Family of God and ministers of the Word, thank you for your commitment toward me and your exemplifying Christ in your lives. I am forever grateful that God allowed our paths to cross.

Alexander Zing Levine for technical assistance with book layout and cover design; your dedication and expertise is highly valued.

Most of all, I wish to express my deepest gratitude and love for my husband, Don Evans, and my parents, George and Ruby Sharp, who loved and inspired me to follow my dreams.

Foreword

By Annette Evans, Founder, SAINTSofGOLD

*Oh Lord, how long shall I cry and You will
Not hear? Even cry out to You, "Violence!"
And You will not save.*

Habakkuk 1:1

It has been a series of divine steps that have led to the writing of this book. I didn't realize that my interests would lead me to think about and even discuss the fundamental aspects of economics, politics, theology and psychology and the philosophy behind these subjects, and not necessarily in this order, nor to cover all the topics in this, my first book…so possibly I will be writing again. This book is intended for those who specifically know they need more power as a saint. This title may cause confusion and misunderstanding as to who really are saints. Some may even think or consider it as sacrilegious to call those who know God saints. Nevertheless, if you have accepted and received the gift of salvation through Jesus, you are called a saint. It is hopeful intent thereby to present a reminder of the authority and power which you have and should walk in.

Because there is an increasing spirit of anti-Christ that prevails upon the land, it is time for saints to rise up. The harvest is truly great and we can no longer be few in number with our voices and actions in demonstrating courage and bravery in resisting the changes that are rapidly occurring. Secular humanism is being shoved and force-fed to the saint with aggression. God says it's not about us, but it's about proclaiming the name of Jesus. We must not be intimidated by that name, which we represent. We must stay the course and not turn back. The saints must fight the good fight of faith, moving strategically through prayer first, then action. It is imperative that we collectively come together with a sense of urgency to assault, not in a literal sense; but this assault is of a spiritual nature to make a phenomenal impact to those that resist the truth.

Whether saints realize it or not, we are under great attack in our economics, politics, theologies, psychologies, and other thoughts of ideologies as well. Saints are in a cultural war with the world, and unfortunately many have not been properly trained for warfare, or have not taken their training seriously. In the meantime, things began to change very subtly to the point of not protecting our children, our homes, churches, places of employment, and the secular society began calling the shots. We ignored the changes and became even intimidated to speak up about them. So the war didn't just begin; it has, however, begun to intensify here in America. Already around the world, there are several concentrated areas of intensity, which has uprooted and destroyed the lives of many. For those of you who have literally fought wars and been in combat around the world, thank you so much for your continued service for justice and freedom, specifically here in America.

The body of Christ will hopefully begin to wake up to the reality of what we as saints are dealing with in our Western culture: a rebellious and wicked society. We are to become again one nation under God and fight for the sake of what we believe in and what we disagree with. We believe in the cross of Christ. If you don't know what that means, you may not in fact be one of us saints. Recognize we are in a culture that is resistant to anything that is lovely, pure and good. Understand and believe that we do not wrestle against flesh and blood, so I say it like this, that people are being negatively influenced by spiritual principalities, which are demonic, in lower and higher command posts of authority, i.e., generals and admirals, and foot soldiers, just as in our national active military hierarchy; all of whom take orders from a spiritual commander in chief, Satan, the adversary. There is no difference with the orders given by our president, who is the Commander-In-Chief.

Do you believe this? This must be our first order of business: Do you believe? The battle is not ours, it is our God, but we must keep marching on to assist in gaining more lives and territories, which matters for the Kingdom's sake. We must not become disinterested, disengaged, develop apathy or become discouraged. We cannot get weary in our actions, thinking our efforts are useless and having feelings of despair and hopelessness.

Too many saints have led quiet, passive, and uncontested lives on our jobs, in our homes and churches; but at what cost to the culture and the church today? It seems we have even become more passive and quiet, confused and disoriented as saints in today's society. Our public voices are being drowned out by the voices of those who truly do not care about others, but only pretend to care for selfish and egotistical gains. Unfortunately, the saints sometimes demonstrate these similar characteristic traits, which must now be challenged.

Have we somehow forgotten just who we are? Have we as saints come to a stalemate of indifference, too afraid to address our concerns in the public market place, let alone in our homes, schools, and churches? Are we intimidated to take a position of truth, love and hope for those we know and care about first, and to others? How effective do you think you are to those around you if you are a saint? Do you realize the high calling which has been given to you as a saint? To much is given, much is due.

No one generation is necessarily being identified as failing the next in a lackadaisical manner of not being godly examples when demonstrating and communicating biblical truths to the generations of Zs, Millennials or Xs and Baby Boomers; the names are not the focus. What is the focus is when rebellious and disobedient people choose to resist and ignore biblical truths of God Almighty, and treat biblical truths as fairy tales and myths, what will be the outcome? Of course, if you have read your Bible, you understand that the scripture says, "Evil men and imposters will grow worse and worse, deceiving and being deceived." Saints have always played a role in a disinterested culture rebelling against the truth of God. Remember we, too, were once disinterested and rebellious toward God. We are now ambassadors for positive change, overcoming resistance and rebellion because that's what obedient saints do. We have to be different. The man and woman of God who has become contaminated with things that are now overflowing in unrighteous, ungodliness, without affection, no virtue, without truth, and without godly love, have to examine themselves.

Immorality and dishonesty is more acceptable for the saints who should know better, but yet settle for these faults within and from others. Don't be deceived; are you truly one of us? Many Saints have become less and less interested in biblical truths and doctrines, but attracted to cultural ideologies, mythologies and lies. Are you one who seeks out many things other than the word of God? We seek out preachers and teachers whose sermons have become fickle with a tickle. Our religious programs constantly change when previous ones didn't seem to attract, forgetting to focus on growing and strengthening those who attend and are committed wholeheartedly. Many of the sermons and illustrations, which are not convicting, tend to be soothing and nonthreatening, making us laugh and feel good about ourselves and our accomplishments. Doctrines are scaled down and talked about very little if at all. Even the word 'hell' seems to be a taboo and unmentionable.

Read this book with objectivity and a call to action as a saint in a changing and uncertain and hostile world. The outlook for saints should be one of hope and love, one that's inclusive but yet exclusive.

Introduction

*Look among the nations and watch—
be utterly astounded! For I will work in
your days which you would not believe,
though it were told you.*

Habakkuk 1:5

I believe that the Spirit of God has given me an opportunity through this book to challenge the saints of God. The name itself, **SAINTSofGOLD**, has many connotations, one being precious metal... gold; another is the Olympic Games where athletes compete to win the gold. Two other allegories are the spiritual maturity of the saint which is meant by the 'golden years', and of course let's not forget 'money' itself, gold.

We have to rise up with a standard like gold in this 21st century. We are at present experiencing more unjust and unfair treatment of all sorts. While saints are sitting together at churches and other gatherings debating the truths of the Bible, many non believers are not even being invited to any kind of saintly gathering or social outing. Many around the world are not even allowed to gather as saints. Persecutions are very real and serious and are not noticeable in our world, in America.

We are not as of yet subjected to extreme hatred and killings with limited Bibles and information about how to remain faithful and at peace. Yet other saints in other parts of the world are making a profound impact on lives with the good news of the gospel, without the comforts and ease we are so accustomed to. They do so sometimes even unto death. I'm not there yet, either. But Saints, ask yourself, "When was the last time I gave someone the gospel and actually talked them through the salvation message?"

Saints will come through the fire with brilliance through purification only if they are willing to stay in the fire. Saints of old were burned at the stake, slaughtered and beaten, used as human torches, thrown in ancient arenas for entertainment, beheaded and crucified. Saints here in America do not know these things, and it is certainly my prayer that we will never know. But are you ready to stand up for the truth of

God? Do you believe you can make a difference by taking a stand for righteousness?

The first century apostles and believers took a message of the cross to a dying and degenerate world. They did not realize how much they would have to jeopardize in order to spread and offer their compelling message given them by Jesus himself. However, the persecution that was suffered by them was worth it all. They gave their lives to sustain their belief. They gave their all to keep the message of hope alive.

Still today millions and millions believe that message of hope, and fortunately are willing to give their lives for it. The message continues to be spread around the world. They stood firm to the truth of what they believed to their dying breath. The apostle Paul in the Bible was a fervent messenger, even to his death. He wrote over two-thirds of the New Testament. Are you willing to stand firm to what you believe for the sake of the cross? For the sake of your family? Please certainly don't be the hypocrite, like many then and now. Realize your weaknesses in standing firm and seek help from committed and faithful others to come along side you.

This book was written to bring attention primarily to those of us called saints. It will hopefully help to identify what is grabbing our attention and causing us to lose perspective of the most important thing in life… love. We are to first love God, one another (saints); then love the enemy, love the hater and pray for those who do not know or believe in the truth of God, that their hearts and minds will open and become receptive to His Truth.

For those who are at least 50 or older, the dramatic changes in our culture have been startling and unbelievable, if you think like me. The question is, "How much of the changes have you accepted?" Saints should be appalled by actions against God across all institutions. This is a critical juncture for our nation and the world where the defining lines have to be drawn to snatch people out of the wiles of the enemy; literally out of Hell. Wrong can no longer be right, and right can no longer be wrong. Dishonesty and integrity do not go together, they are not synonymous; your heart can hold no place for one when you harbor the other.

Wishing you the fullness of God's blessings as a Saint of Gold, Annette.

Table of Contents

Foreword	ix
Introduction	xiii
Chapter 1: Believing in a Sovereign God	1
Chapter 2: Take a Closer Look	18
Chapter 3: Where Have You Dropped Off Your Faith?	34
Chapter 4: Let the Saints Come Out of the Closet!	42
Chapter 5: False or Fact?	54
Chapter 6: Enemies Within	67
Chapter 7: Don't Be Caught Without This	81
Chapter 8: I Know Better but No One Saw Me	90
Chapter 9: Someone's Watching Us	101
Chapter 10: The Gold Standard… What Is It?	114

Chapter 1

Believing in a Sovereign God

My Story

Everyone has a story and this is mine. It doesn't matter where you come from, but at some point, as with most people, I came to respect and care about my roots, particularly my spiritual roots. I wanted to reflect on the inheritance and the significance of my family's story and how it helped shape my belief in a sovereign God.

My mom and dad were Christians. They weren't born Christians because nobody can be born a Christian, and they became Christian by choice and practice. My dad came from a big family of 12. He had eight brothers and three sisters. His father, my grandfather, died young, so his mom had to raise their children all by herself in rural Mississippi during the depression in the 1920s. Of course hardships for blacks were normal with discriminatory and segregation laws, so the effects of that time were different for my parents. They managed as they always did, through farming and service work among themselves and for others. My paternal grandmother was stern and very spiritual, and powerful with praying. It was a must for her with eight sons to raise alone in the South, so my dad and his family grew up as firm believers in the teachings of God, the power of prayer and the sovereignty of God.

My mom's family also provided a strong religious setting, and my maternal grandmother's strong faith was the foundation of her family, too. My mom was the oldest of seven children and she had five brothers and one sister, all of which were influenced by her due to her love for God early on in life. She demonstrated a lot of patience toward her family.

Both of my parents grew up in a family environment that taught them about the God of the Bible and the death, burial and resurrection of Jesus. They grew up with the understanding and knowledge of the Bible's teachings, and so my siblings and I didn't have a choice of knowing anything else but the Word of God and love for Jesus during our adolescent years. My parents had 10 children, four boys and six girls. My mom was a stay-at-home mom, and found ways to bring in additional monies to help my dad provide for us. I remember, when

I was eight or nine years old, she worked outside our home at the home of a Jewish doctor. This family was very nice to us, and my mom worked there for several years part-time with the doctor's family. As we got older, my mom began working a full-time job. My mom was a woman of excellence and trained her children to be responsible, reliable, and dependable, and to have a spirit of excellence as well.

Because of my training, at an early age I would get up and help my sisters and brothers get ready for school, make their breakfast, and comb their hair. They were much younger, so I also remember changing diapers. They didn't have Pampers back then! You had to first swoosh-out the diapers in the toilet if #2, and then wash them clean. My mom and dad didn't have a lot of money so they didn't have the amenities other people had like washers and dryers and those kinds of things. We had a wringer washer and it would agitate the clothes, so at least we didn't have to wash them by hand with the scrub board, although she had once used it and still had it on hand. Once the clothing was washed, we hung the laundry outdoors on the line.

I remember those hard days for my mom, but they were never hard or bad days for me. They were days that were busy with taking care of my younger siblings, going to school, and learning about the sovereignty of God and what it meant that Jesus died for me, from my father's many Bible sermons, teachings, and discussions. As a child I simply observed the love and commitment they both had toward one another and toward God. I saw my dad's strength and perseverance to lead, guide and provide for his family and my mom's courageous spirit of excellence in helping him. They were consistent and genuine in sharing their love and faith in a sovereign God, and the goodness of that faith with their children and others.

Church was a very big part of my upbringing, and it seemed like we were going to church every day. Maybe it wasn't every day, but it certainly seemed that way. It felt like we were always in church, praying, singing, reading and studying, and shouting. I didn't mind this as a kid. It was my desire to be with my parents, and if it meant church, I was okay with it.

I remember teaching my younger brothers and sisters Sunday lessons when I was eight years old. I actually began my teaching career as a Sunday school teacher for the kids that were younger than I was, like five, six and seven-year-olds. I was only eight or nine and I was teaching Sunday school lessons. I knew the Bible stories from top to bottom because we focused on the stories in the Bible throughout my adolescent years. My dad loved the Old Testament stories, and seemed to drill them into our memory. What a dad! He helped us see and understand the character flaws of the men and women of the Bible, and how they were no different than us when obeying or disobeying a sovereign God. Obedience toward God always brings about positive change and growth when applying His biblical principles. I got so much out of the stories, and there's so much that crosses over into everyday life applications. There is a wealth of information and guidance in how these stories can apply in our daily lives.

My father was a barber and my mother a part-time hairdresser in our home. Talk about a Proverbs 31 woman – which she was. As far as I'm concerned, they were community activists. My mom would do press and curl, pressing women's hair with a hot straightening comb and then curling it with a hot curling iron. This is how it was done for many women of color back in those days. This was something she learned when she was growing up and she did it whenever she needed additional money. She did many heads of hair, mostly on weekends, and was additionally busy during the week training and teaching me and my siblings to be decent God-fearing people. My siblings and I saw her and my dad as kind of community counselors. We knew they would share biblical principles of living Godly every chance they got. Dad would talk to the men, most of which had wives, about living clean and decent lives as he cut their hair, and about the different domestic situations and life issues they faced, that we knew nothing about. I saw how my parents engaged with these people. There were stories about the women we knew living with alcoholics, wife abusers or adulterers.

My parents were able to counsel these people according to the Word of God to the best of their knowledge and understanding. They had a knack for this. This was my perspective growing up, witnessing how my parents were involved with the people in our community and I've always been appreciative of the values I learned by watching them. That's what children do, watch and learn from parental guidance, good, bad, or ugly.

I grew up in the '70s and elementary and middle schools were very safe and conservative then. I remember we were not allowed to wear slacks and required to wear skirts. One day as usual I went to school wearing slacks under my skirt because of the cold winter months. Somehow the dress code rules changed that day and allowed girls to wear slacks outright. I just whipped off that skirt and now I had the pants on. This was so neat! As I think about it now, it had to do with the women's rights movement, progressively making headway for the 'new and liberated woman.' Things were definitely changing for women and the nation in the '70s. People were beginning to move away from the belief in a sovereign God and biblical principles of that belief. Also, Afros were a big trend then, after the political activists of the '60s, but my mom wouldn't allow us to wear our hair in an Afro because she didn't want us to look unpresentable. Later she gave in and allowed us girls to wear Afros. I had an Afro in the 7th grade, and I was proud of it. The trend has definitely made a comeback!

My mom and dad, I think, were progressives for the era in which I grew up, the '60s and '70s, because a lot of children growing up in Christian homes couldn't do what we were able to do. Our parents chose to be a little less conservative when it came to bringing us up in a changing world. I was glad they allowed us to play sports, and participate in activities in and out of school. It was good for us not to be so restricted, and helped break the routines of regularly having to go to church. As a teenager of about 13, my older siblings and I had a weekly ritual of going skating every Monday night. Black people from around the community, in a radius of 10-30 miles, would come together for an outing of fun, skating, and music from the latest Motown hits. Mom and dad tried to shield us as much as possible from the challenges occurring in the world, particularly in the south for Blacks during that time. They compromised some to help us grow up during the changes. My parents however, always reminded us of who we represented, which was God, and how to live Godly in our everyday lives.

I'm from a small town in Indiana. There was only one high school in the area at the time I graduated, and students from many different areas of the county attended there. My graduating class was about 670 students and only eight of us were black. As I got older and looked back, I understood why my experiences and outlook as a black teenager and young adult was slightly prejudiced. I understood to some extent the struggles and injustices of the black experiences, and some of the racial tensions that were occurring at the time as a nation. However, I really hadn't experienced racism in a personal way until my memorable first encounter. I was denied an apartment after graduating because I was black. The sound of my voice on the phone was okay for availability, but once seen…'Rented'. My mom and dad put some emphasis on race relations, but made sure we understood the underlying core issue of man's evil and wicked heart, a reminder of believing in a sovereign God.

Unlike today, there wasn't nearly as much of a national sensitivity and heightened consciousness about ethnicity, culture and racism as today. However, in the South it was different. I remember the bombing and killings of the little black girls at the church, the dogs being loosed and water hoses being sprayed on men, women and children in the marches of the South and much more. It was common for racism issues to be discussed from church pulpits occasionally.

These social and political issues were also discussed at the local community centers where Blacks gathered, and of course in families. I'm sure my parents had discussions on race and injustices with the people to whom they provided services. As children, we were getting older as well and had questions we felt needed answers about the uneasiness of our nation about black people. My parents focused on society as a whole, the heart of man, and the good and evil deeds of man. They seemed to see everything from the perspective of God's biblical principles and the belief that those principles were true.

Color was not the issue, but having a heart of righteousness or evil, either wanting to do right or do wrong, either good or bad, that was the real issue of man. Going into high school and becoming more aware of our society caused me to begin to believe that their biblical perspectives seemed shallow and insignificant for those issues at that time. I now fully understand the approach they took, and the heart condition of man is the core issue today. It always has been and will be, until it is changed by a sovereign God.

In our small community people seemed divided, but the division was according to income, not skin color. Whites and Blacks lived together in my community, however the area I grew up in was mostly concentrated with aunts and uncles and a few other black families. There were a few other ethnicities scattered throughout our small community. I remember a doctor who lived in a very posh neighborhood. His status afforded him and his family better housing. His skin color possibly helped his living conditions as well. As Blacks we note 'light complexion-dark complexion', and 'passing'. He didn't look 'black'. My parents seemed unphased by negative remarks and prejudices of this family. My eldest brother actually dated one of the daughters.

I learned so many valuable lessons by observing my mother and father in their interactions with people of all kinds and absorbing their communication skills. My biggest take-away from them is: the quality of a person is not contingent upon status, skin color, or financial worth, but on the amount of compassion, care and concern given to others, particularly those who are neglected, weak, and treated unfairly. It all boils down to love God, and love your neighbor as yourself.

Having the heart to care for people ... it's this trait that I am most thankful God has helped me develop over the years. Having a love for people is what my parents taught most, first starting with family. Being loving, kind, encouraging and patient toward others is not always easy.

This book is about Saints, who will give more, take less, help more, complain less, and stand up for the cause of the Bible. It is a reminder to keep believing in a sovereign God that knows our past, present and future. We are to love God and are loved by God, we are to love one another, and we are to give hope for the good news of the truths of the Bible to all.

Stories of Others

Because our eyes should be open, as saints we will often see people suffering in some form or other, and they need our support, encouragement, and our love. Frankly, we all need to be helping each other whether saints or not. People are going through all kinds of difficult life experiences. Some are momentary and some are life-long. Here's a story about a former boss of mine that shows how a saint could walk alongside someone in their time of need, and serve someone under duress in a work environment.

I've had many different jobs in the course of my life. Some were just temporary to bring home a paycheck, and some were career-level jobs. Now that I have time to look back on them, I see how God was weaving my life into the fabric of other people's lives with each employment experience. I see the hand of God bringing people and situations to me so I could become increasingly capable of doing His plan and purpose which He has for all.

This incident took place in a small office with just five employees. It was one of the first retail computer stores at that time. This computer store was growing very quickly, becoming a competitive corporation at the time when desktop computers were first becoming popular. My boss got a phone call one afternoon and suddenly became completely upset. He grew red-faced and I could see he was almost out of control with anger and fear. He had been in the retail area of the store and when one of the sales people made a comment, he blew up, becoming out of control as the store manager. He rushed back to his office, slammed the door, and we could hear him yelling through the walls.

We were all stunned and didn't know what to do. Someone said, "One of us needs to go back to his office and check on him." "Not me, not me," said another. "I will," I said. I began to think he might hurt himself, he was so distraught, so I told the others I was going back to talk to him and see if he was okay.

I knocked on the door and he said to come in. I said, "Are you okay?" and he said he was but I could see that this was merely words. We began to talk a bit and that's when he revealed the situation. The phone call informed him that the store was closing. As he told me, he began to weep and I was thinking, "Oh, my God, this guy is crying!" When I saw that, I said soothing and encouraging words to comfort him and later in the day he was okay and the store returned to normal.

Realizing what happened and how God had used me to calm things down, I said a quick prayer. "Wow! Thank you, Lord. Thank you for making me the person you made me to be." God makes all of us with the capacity for love and compassion, with the ability to provide caring and kindness toward others. Whether or not we can cultivate this ability and make it available to people when something goes wrong, that's up to us. A Saint of Gold will step forward and look for ways to ease a broken heart or calm a frightening moment filled with fear.

I don't know if my boss was a Believer or not, but I was. I believe that God gives all of us the capacity within our being to love and care for others. That love and caring we carry in our hearts simply needs to be cultivated, especially in the young, as soon as possible. As a human being on a spiritual journey, our base-self is focused on things of this world, on our survival, and on our desire to have more for our self at the expense of others. As a Saint of Gold, God puts a yearning for Him in our hearts and the knowledge of correct action. It's all His doing according to our willingness. When we carry God's message in our hearts, and we act on it in the daily events and situations we encounter, we become better servants of God's Will.

Other Saints

I have another story to tell about a very nice elderly man and his wife whom I met by coincidence. They were an interracial couple and his wife was from Denmark. Apparently they had some difficult and hard times in life, as we all do. I later came to understand that God had placed me in their lives to help them begin to have trust with people again. I was young and they were at least 40 years my senior. At first it was very difficult to be with them because they were both rather crabby and mistrusting of me. The woman had been very prominent when she was growing up in Denmark, and he had been a popular musician in France in the '40s and '50s. The three of us became friends and I got them to attend church regularly, and also to begin discussing ideas about God and that God sent His son Jesus to the world for us. As time went on, the three of us became very close and they treated me like I was their daughter.

Because of my influence, the older gentleman began going to church regularly. His wife attended too, but she was rather sickly and she went when she could. I would help him go to church and would drive out of my way to pick him up, take him to church, take him home, and then drive back to my home in a different city. Though it was out of my way, I wanted to make sure he was receiving the Word of God and growing in his faith. Not only that, but since he was a musician, he began playing the keyboard for the church and became very active in the church's events. Everyone at the church liked him.

Sure enough, he became more and more interested, and the Spirit of the Lord touched him and inspired him to read the Bible and become proficient. At first he would fumble through the Bible and try to find the Bible chapters. I noticed he would have a difficult time, and he allowed me to assist him. A lot of people are prideful and don't want to act like they don't know what they're doing, but he would allow me to help him and he started growing as a student and a believer. He would go home and do research and the next thing you knew, he could find the passages read by the pastor. I could see his growth, and I was so excited by the sight of this and felt privileged to experience his own excitement. Imagine the thought of God smiling at you in the small ways of helping others. I was so excited for him. He began to grow even stronger in his knowledge and faith, and our conversations changed, composed now of mature conversations about God and Jesus and the role of mankind.

It wasn't long before I had to make some life changes that disrupted my ability to take him to church on a regular basis. I couldn't believe that God was sending me someplace else and I wondered who was going to help and escort this wonderful elderly man to church.

As it turned out, no one did. He stopped going to church. My new circumstances would no longer allow me to take him anymore, but I knew he was in someone's path, and someone could have stepped up and helped him get to church, but they didn't.

This was very sad to me. I found it hard to believe there wasn't one person in the church who could help him, or that a group of people would, together, figure out a way to offer scheduled rides. Why weren't we…why aren't we… more supportive to each other? Why don't we see our obligation to help our brothers and sisters, our fathers and mothers? Why do we let ourselves forget our responsibility to others, to God, to our true nature as a believer, as a Christian, as a true Saint of Gold!

The church and its members neglected him. He died. His wife died first. Her sister had difficulty even supporting her at death. I knew it was a heart of unforgiveness due to the hurt she'd carried for many years. However, the saints weren't there for either of them, at least not in a way that I really hoped and expected.

Strangers came to help but where were the church people? When he died, I was the first person to be called and told he was dying. I went to him and I was with him when he died. He was okay that he was dying. He knew in his heart that his heart belonged to Jesus and everything was okay. He had a very peaceful death.

Then the pastor and his wife showed up. They said, "What are we going to do about this? Who is his family?"

I said, "You're his family." They looked at me and shrugged me off. I ended up having a service for him at a different church, the church I was now attending. The pastor and his wife didn't want to attend but they came, and they sat in the back. They didn't want to say anything on his behalf even though he had been a member of their church, and even a musical participant. It was quite shameful that they weren't carrying out God's love and care for their brother as sheep of their flock. They were empty in their hearts. The light and love of Jesus was absent from them during that particular situation. Thank God for His mercy and grace.

The lesson here is to be mindful of our actions, and prayerful of others who are not mindful of their actions. First of all, know that you truly are a saint of God, with gold standard intentions. Know you're golden in your heart. Make an impact first in your life so God can say, "Well done." Secondly, know that your gold will spill over into the lives of others. Know that we need to do better. We need to be deserving of being called Saints and not have the world look at us as though we are tainted…tainted saints.

Society in General

The social and cultural messages the media broadcasts today are extreme, and I believe this is very unhealthy for people, young and old. The media very strongly influences how we raise our children, how we view societal changes, what foods we eat and clothes we wear. For some reason, parents regard television as a form of entertainment and don't exercise sufficient supervision or restrictions on what their children can watch. Because of this neglect, and because of a lack of public accountability, the media has exerted more and more negative influence on our young people and even on those of us from yesteryears.

Today's society is so much different than it was just 10 and 20 years ago. Of course, we don't want to get stuck in the past, but we have to find a way to use media in a positive and healthy way that is encouraging and uplifting. With the kind of information disseminated, the information we're being shown and hearing somehow affects the way we think, which has been proven statistically. Many have become complacent and accept that this information will not affect them, but the steady stream of negative news is not healthy for us. These highly negative influences are magnified by the corollary messaging we constantly receive on our computers through the Internet.

When I worked for the computer retailer some 30 years ago, it was a major computer store growing quickly. This was before Microsoft was on the scene. This retailer was on the cutting edge then, the number one computer store, introducing the IBM PC in the early '80s but soon Microsoft had grabbed the market and computer technology competition began, eventually causing this company to go out of business way too soon.

Witnessing this quick rise and rapid fall, it was difficult to grasp how a giant company could suddenly disappear. But because of my religious upbringing, I certainly began to ponder these kinds of occurrences beginning to happen in the business world and how they could possibly relate to the Bible. I really didn't understand at that time the impact that computers and the Internet would have today.

Does anyone know where technology is taking us? With the Internet, everyone is connected to this giant and influential network where everything is accessible. Today, kids have mobile phones that connect them directly with the Internet, and who knows what content these impressionable young minds are viewing? Is the information appropriate for their age? Are monitoring and discussions occurring frequently within families, churches, and schools?

Most children, adolescents, teenagers, and young adults have access to information and materials that undermine the establishment and undermine the biblical foundation. The information our youth is exposed to often deviates from the teachings of the Bible, from the teachings of God. Whether you want to believe this or not, God is sovereign, which means that God is supreme, He is all knowing, all seeing, and over all. It's His world, this world is His creation, and we are here to serve His wishes. Much of the material our youth is viewing is contrary to the development of healthy minds and hearts, and leads people away from believing in a Sovereign God. Let us remember that God is Almighty and everything belongs to Him.

Attitudes

Yes, many things have changed, and the Sovereignty of God expected the changes. The attitudes of the culture in the '60s and '70s, of the Baby Boomers, it's definitely different now. Did this generation expect this kind of change? We've gone through a lot in the intervening years with all the deception and non-truth that's been disseminated and accelerated. The devil is a liar, and the devil finds ways to spread non-truth. Lies have become truths and truths are lies, and you get all distracted and mixed up. What may be true then may not necessarily be true now. The good may be bad, the bad may be good. It's so confusing! But do not be disheartened. There is hope in someone. I hope that's you.

I am grateful to share my story, but it's not just my story, it's a story for everyone. Maybe you didn't grow up in a Christian family, but the Truth is out there for everyone to see, know and have. Hopefully my story will inspire you to seek the Truth. The Truth is the one thing people can hold onto in times of need and times like these. Faith will enable people and you to conform, renew and transform in a good, positive and healthy way that's pleasing to a Sovereign God.

The culture has indeed changed. It's good for those who can see the changes in society like some of my young adult friends and family (21 – 36 years old). Thankfully they can see immense changes in just the last five years of their young lives. Children have to rely on their parents to talk about the changes happening in our culture. Maybe parents haven't talked about the past so they're unable to talk about the future. Maybe parents haven't been expressing the things that are good and the things that are not right. Maybe parents haven't talked about these things because they are content with how things are now, and are accepting there is less biblical connection.

A lot of people struggle with these kinds of discussions and the transparency of their own mistakes and shortcomings of life; but there are no excuses. No excuses! It is the responsibility of parents to talk about the past and compare it with the present so they can help their children see and prepare for a brighter and meaningful future. The children are our future. Parents should educate their children about the things that are good and the things that are not right. Every person, all of us, should not just accept what society has declared is good or bad. Parents and their children need to be guided by the Truth, the Truth that is in the Bible.

When I talk about Saints of Gold there were several transforming thoughts given me, I believe, from God about the word gold. The word 'gold' means God Offering Love Daily…GOLD. Today, we use the word "love" so generically that it's lost its true meaning. "Love everybody." "Love him." "Love her." "Everybody loves one another." "Let everybody love who they want and just love one another as they are." Expressions like these don't make sense to me given the larger picture, the larger meaning, the meaning of love as it was intended from a divine biblical perspective. Go back to your first love, Saints, that love you felt when you truly gave your heart to God. When you realized you were in sin and practicing sin willfully and needed Him to save you (set you free). We love Him because He first loved us. The misunderstanding about love is evident in our society because it falls rather short of the kind of love Jesus is referencing in His teachings.

When we talk about turmoil, it's the turmoil from within. This turmoil is simply carrying a really bad attitude, and it perpetuates. We sometimes lose our identity of who we truly are and are afraid to discuss who we really have become. No one frequently talks about the innate bad nature of man and the miraculous ability from God to change and improve our bad nature. We fail to see our own value, thereby devaluing others more than what they know. There is hope and there is another life, a better life. It doesn't mean dying to get to the other better life. A better life can be achieved now, today. Believe in a Sovereign God! His plan, His purpose and His benefits for life are amazing and bad attitudes must be eliminated.

Then there is what I call "the orphanage attitude". A lot of children grow up in broken homes, and these children wind up not knowing who they are, not having a decent and strong foundation. They may grow up in foster care or in orphanages. These children are not loved, and they don't feel loved. This can create intense inner turmoil when you feel nobody wants you, nobody cares about you, and you have this deep and hurtful sense of loss, of not feeling love, true love.

What is true love? This is a question that's almost impossible to answer if you grew up in an abusive environment where nobody seems to care about you or anybody. Sadly, we have become less interested in one another and more interested in selfish personal pursuits. Parents have become too busy with life and often neglect their children. The Millennials and Generation X have a different mindset, which has unintentionally been taught to them. They have been taught differently in schools, too. It's up to parents and previous generations of family and friends to uphold the teachings of the past, especially the teachings of the Bible. My father knew all the books of the Bible, and he quoted them, especially the Old Testament from Genesis to Malachi. I was surprised and asked him, "How did you learn that?" He said, "We learned that in school." "Really?" I said. "You learned that in school, book by book?" I was so impressed with him. Nowadays the mere mention of the name of Jesus might get you in trouble at school.

Parents today have an attitude of mistrust and weariness. They're tired of battling and they think they can't win against society, that they can't be victorious against the world's perspective, against a secular system that's against God, against how the world thinks and does things. It is a constant battle and they are bone-weary. They don't have people to join them and help them with their struggles. Come on, Saints, we need one another. We're on a winning team! Let's help each other become better, not bitter, angry, frustrated and exhausted. We believe in a Sovereign God.

Certainly there are books that tend to help and I've read some of them, but I think some self-help books can be very generic. They touch on the topic superficially. They just give advice on what people can do or must do and the emphasis is on prospering. There is nothing wrong with prospering, but many need one-on-one personal care and encouragement step-by-step before handling more. That's love! On top of that, some of these books fail to recognize the emotions of the person who is feeling anger, resentment, loneliness, and the feeling of being abandoned. We need families, mentors, life coaches, counselors, anyone who won't abandon you and will help you get to the next phase of your life, people who will help you realize you have value, you are worthy, and you are loved, and not just through words.

The mistrust in our young people is rampant. They feel disappointed because they have been let down too often. Our word is our bond, so I always tell every young person, "If you tell me something, I want to be able to take it to the bank," as the cliché goes. I want to believe a person's word is reliable and true. Don't you? I've noticed there's a lot of disconnect between the values of the younger and older generations and one reason why these disconnects exist is because we look at one another as objects of gain and sometimes personal gratification. We lack integrity; we become no different than the person who doesn't profess to be a 'saint'. What can he or she do for us? How can I benefit? This is an unhealthy attitude!

For example, one of my younger brothers said to me, "Momma and Daddy did more for Mrs. Scott than they did for me," and I said, "You feel that way because Momma and Daddy were always helping other people…but you weren't lacking in anything." My point is that I think we don't do enough for others, and we don't realize how much others are already doing for us. We want others to do more and more for us, and that's the nature of the society we've created. We want people to serve us and do for us, and if that's what everybody wants, no one benefits.

My Momma and Daddy showed me their heart condition toward loving people unconditionally and I've chosen to develop mine over the years. They taught me to see people where they're at, and be kind and loving toward people. You could in fact be engaging an angel sent by God. I learned to push people forward, without their really knowing they were being prodded a bit. This was the inheritance from my parents, not money.

Tactical Maneuvers

There are tactical maneuvers of the world and there are tactical maneuvers of God. There are two ways to live our life, one using skillful tactics as a servant of God or using the skillful tactics as a servant of the world, (the devil).

The tactics of the world are obviously the love of money, power, cunning, craftiness with deceit and trickery, rebellion, lust…and the list is long. These world tactics are to be expected within the world, but saints too often find ourselves ensnared, too. These tactics can be seen everywhere for both the world and saints. Because of the media today, tablets, cell phones, the Internet and TV with a thousand channels, we've become bombarded with the lifestyles of Hollywood stars, Washington, D.C. powerbrokers and politicians, the NFL, NBA and other sport superstars, business moguls, celebrity musicians and mega-preachers of world celebrity status, rich and famous. The tactics of 'Fools Gold' of the world is prevalent in our society today. All you have to do is turn on your TV set to see the Fool's Gold of the world, advertisements and seductive cultural ideologies, lulling the saints asleep. We mimic their lifestyle, we mimic their appearance, and we want to substitute God's tactics for the world's. Believing in a sovereign God isn't just believing but administering His tactics. We are different, we are Saints of Gold.

When you look a little closer, you find many of the world squandering their fortunes on palaces, costly weddings, multi-million dollar homes, yachts, fancy cars, and wearing costly diamonds, jewels and Rolexes. They are in and out of rehab centers and the courts, on a merry-go-round of marriages and divorces, and living a royal lifestyle by ransoming their souls and living with deceit, lies, and falsehoods with wicked and evil hearts. The tactics of the world imprison minds that choose to live in the darkness of the armor of the world, and sadly people don't know any better. God's tactics provide freedom, protection and security, peace and joy without tainted deceits, lies and falsehoods.

This doesn't mean that saints have to deny having material wealth with nice houses, cars, good jobs and money, so the call is for a gold standard of reverence for God with increased awareness and balance. These material objects and things are not evil of themselves, as they are just things. It's the heart condition drawn to worldly tactical maneuvers that entices and tempts saints from truly knowing and believing in the sovereignty of God's Truth.

Beware Saints! These things do get in the way of healthy loving service; these things do get in the way of a committed, covenant relationship with God. Don't be fooled! It's absurd to think world tactics aren't real and enticing. Tactics of the world are appealing and strategically maneuvered for ambitious and driven saints for materialism, power, recognition, fame and more. These can take over our life and become the focus for living. When there is no intentional strategic maneuvering tactics for God, the world's maneuverings continue to prevail.

Economic Changes

Does history really repeat itself? The definition of economics is "The science that deals with production, distribution and consumption of wealth", and the economists are those who specialize in it. There seems to be somewhat of a disconnect in our society today. You think? The economy of our country has changed drastically in the last 50 years. In the 1980s a bag of groceries cost about $10, and today that same bag of groceries costs about $40. A gallon of gasoline was about $1.27 per gallon and now it's about $2.70 and much higher in some countries. Yes, wages have grown, but now we have single-parent families living near the poverty line, and in homes with two parents, both spouses are likely to have a job to make ends meet. Is the sovereignty of God still at play? I believe so.

I have taken serious notice and interest in the last 10 years of what's occurring in our society and around the world. The last two jobs of my employment began to open my eyes to the business world of finance more than ever before. Economics is what everyone has to deal with even if our understanding is minuscule in the bigger scheme of things. Although I worked for larger corporations and my husband ran a business, my interest wasn't there for many years. However, it had been a dream of mine as a child to own and run my own company some day. I believe in the sovereignty of God. To be totally immersed in economics working in the franchise industry, which produces well over half the employment of our nation, was the most exciting career path in which I could participate.

My husband was so pleased with all that I was learning and taking an interest in, such as the GDP – Gross Domestic Products, SEC –Security Exchange Commission, Federal Reserve System, IMF- International Monetary Fund, Wall Street, investment banking, insurance investments and a bubble economy, starting with the dot.com (tech) bubble in the late 1990s. Along with knowing about some of this, I also took interest in who some of the players were in the field of economics and politics. I couldn't believe I was being enlightened, to say the least. Then came the big bust or bubbles for me to fully become aware, take notice, and understand. It was the housing and banking industries' bubbles between 2007-2009.

The federal government has manipulated the value of the dollar for a while now by first going off the gold standard in the '70s. My most recent recollection of economics was the government injecting billions of dollars of paper money into our economic system by introducing Quantitative Easing to adjust economic strains and relations. The tactical maneuvers of the world are always in flow, changing to some new program or system that best serves itself. Compare this with the sovereignty of God and His tactics and believing that His maneuvers never change and are solid and incorruptible.

PRAYER:

> *Father in Heaven, you have made the world and everything in it. You are great and greatly to be praised. Who can understand Your magnificence and power? You are the sovereign God. You are a Holy God. You are a righteous, loving and good God. Because of who You are, let the Saints give You praise. Thank You that we have the privilege of calling You Abba Father. Help us realize the importance of loving You and keeping Your commandments. Your ways and thoughts are higher than our finite minds and we cannot fathom Your infinite wisdom. I pray that as Saints of Gold we will truly begin to rise up to a higher standard in all areas of our lives, which You have called us all to do, because we believe in You.*
>
> *In Jesus' Name I pray.*

Chapter 2

Take a Closer Look

Why Are You Here?

For whatever reason and only God knows, because God knows everything, we grow up in certain environments. It's God given. I know it's difficult to believe. We can be children and grow up in a healthy home environment, or we can be children and grow up in a family of drug users and alcoholics or with verbal or sexual abusers. If such is the case and a child is in this type of home environment all the way to adolescence, at some point they will be able to look at their life and see that their experience has been terrible. Then, when they recognize their situation, they have the conscious choice to continue down that same path or make changes that improves their life. They can go this way or that way.

Some children reach the age of accountability as young as eight or nine, and children this intelligent start asking a lot of questions like, "Why am I here?" Unfortunately, young lives that have been reared by adults with deviant behaviors regarding love would feel empty and alone and would wonder even more, "Why am I here?"

If moms or dads weren't able to help them understand the basics of life through biblical perspectives early on, they might not understand for a very long time, maybe 10 or even 20 years out. When you look at some of the elements in our youth culture, it's easy to see a kind of mindlessness. Many of the images and messages our children look at and listen to don't have the foundation of rational thought. Our young black men are even more affected, unfortunately, by the misguiding of nurture, care and love in their childhood years. Our penal system is proof of this.

Without healthy guidance, people who grow up like this develop hardness and an atheistic mindset that there is no God, and thereby have no value for life or the life of others. For a child growing up in this environment, it's probably very hard to understand and believe there is a God when everything seems so disjointed and random so spiritually purposeless.

However, a child who grows up in a healthy home environment at least has the benefit of living in an environment that has rational thought, where cognitive thinking is regularly used, and love isn't so distorted and perverse. These children usually arrive at the conclusion that there is a rational and discernible purpose for why they exist and why they, and all of us, are here. Why are we here? Because God said we should be here for this time.

Clues Along the Way

There is actual evidence for why we are here and you can find clues along the way. God has created us to have a desire to want to know Him, and this is not by chance.

The problem is that if, for example, I don't believe that God is sovereign, and I don't believe that God is omnipotent, and all the other things that go along with the strong foundation of Christian belief, then who is going to help me appreciate the value of this, and know and accept the importance of this as an active element in my life? The books I might be reading may not be sufficient, the messages I'm seeing or hearing on my daily walk in life might not lead me down the right path or may not be sufficiently transparent for me to see the universal good that otherwise, with proper guidance in my youth, would be self-evident. On the other hand, if I'm tuning into the Dark Side, I may never see the clues and find my way to God. It is the will of God that none should perish, but many will.

From what I've noticed, people get caught up with superficial concerns which distract a person from having a more meaningful relationship that's possible with almost everyone. Unfortunately, the first thing we notice about someone is their physical appearance, and this establishes our initial judgments which will probably be faulty. Are they Black or White, Asian, Hispanic or Native Americans? Are they fat or thin? Short or tall? Clean or dirty? Are they attractive or average or unappealing? Are they book smart or street smart? Nerd or hip?

How do we address the issues of race and shape and sizes of people? People feel unhappy when they are overweight, or not as well dressed as another, or not as handsome or pretty as some. How do we understand these issues without letting them interfere with our acceptance of them, and with our establishing a respectful relationship?

Let me ask you a question. Why would God allow or assign His child, a soul, to live a life as disabled or disfigured, or follow a path as an overweight person, or to live life as a person whose skin color is different, or who lives in poverty, which sets them on a life path as a minority or someone who is socially unacceptable? Why are certain souls given this type of life assignment, and not a different life assignment on Earth?

First, let's define the meaning of the word "soul". The soul is our mind, our will, and our emotions. That's the soul. Everyone has this. It's the basic canvas of our existence, you might say.

Now let's pretend we're all painters in kindergarten. We all have this clean canvas, and there is no good and no bad to the work we will do. Here are the paintbrushes, here is the paint and the smocks, and all the little kindergartners can now just go at it and paint whatever they wish. We have an hour for this painting exercise, and it's our time to paint whatever we like.

When the hour is over, all the little kids look at their painting, and then they look at everybody else's painting. They start to compare, and some of these little Rembrandts get the feeling that their work is less than somebody else's. Comparison leads to judgment and judgment usually leads to "I'm not worthy." This self-assessment starts at a very young age when children begin to compare themselves to other children. "My stuff isn't as good as your stuff." "I'm not as good…as smart…as pretty…as fast…as well-dressed…" These self-assessments, when uncultivated, spill over into many adult lives making the clues more difficult due to pride.

It's so much easier when we only have the soul issue before us because then we can, and God can, cultivate this aspect of our deeper self as opposed to looking at the outward and relatively insignificant appearances of color, size, and intellect. It is the heart condition that needs to be changed through discussion by God.

Your nose is big, your lips are full, and you're a size 22 instead of a 4… God doesn't look at our outward appearances, thank God…and neither should we as saints. People should follow God's lead and stop doing this to ourselves and to each other, and allow every person to blossom and be the soul that they are destined to be, that whole soul-person that God has created each and every one of us to be. There is a reason why souls are assigned the variety of characteristics, and it's not for us to question why these differences exist, but it is our responsibility as Saints of Gold to accept, without judgment, the people who cross our path in life, recognizing them as representations of God's Will on

Earth. Then it is our duty to claim them into the family as a brother or sister and do what we can to help them on their path of reaching God's divine destinies and shelter them and be sheltered by them with love.

What Is My Purpose?

Why are we here and what is our purpose?

First of all, we are here to love God and to love one another. That's our essential purpose.

As I've mentioned, there are clues along the way, and maybe you missed some growing up as a child. Can you still find them? Yes, of course you can. Matthew 7:7, "…seek and you will find".

Well, what are you seeking? If you don't know, someone needs to help you. Are you seeking for the right things? You'll know because you'll feel it in your spirit, which is your conscience. You know if it's right or wrong and it's rather interesting how we're wired to know the truth. We might reject it, perhaps, but we know it.

I used to question myself and ask, "What is my purpose?" I know now my main purpose is to serve God and serve others. If you're not serving God or serving others, then you're off-purpose. When we are serving God and serving others, it's done with love.

The idea of writing this book came to me one day, and of course the idea was inspired by God. As I thought about the book over a period of time, I heard the title, **SAINTSOFGOLD**. I was asking God why **SAINTSOFGOLD**? I didn't come up with that name. I tried to ignore it, actually! I had a list of other titles I'd written about three years ago, and an associate helped me choose another title. I changed **SAINTSOFGOLD** to this other title, and then later the Lord said, "I said **SAINTSOFGOLD**." Really, Lord? Okay, so I changed the title back to **SAINTSOFGOLD**.

As I spoke with people about my book and its title, I found people were very curious about what the title meant. As I thought about it, I realized that the mineral, gold, was a metaphor for something more. I asked myself about the purpose of gold and I remembered that when gold is mined, it has to go through a purification process. I also remember that people want gold because it's appealing to the eye, and I even reflected on athletes entering the Olympics to win a gold medal. Then I began thinking about how God giving His love equated with

Saints being gold. I read something that said "of all minerals, none is more useful than gold". I thought about that, and then began to think about gold's spiritual aspect. That's when I found this passage:

"…gold continues to play its ancient role as the only true standard of value in times of war or crisis. … History tells us that only gold retains its value during wars and upheavals, changes of empires and governments, and times of crisis. …gold is the oldest and most respected currency in the world …" [1]

And then I also found this one:

"Of all the minerals mined from the Earth, none is more useful than gold. Its usefulness is derived from a diversity of special properties. Gold conducts electricity, does not tarnish, is very easy to work, can be drawn into wire, can be hammered into thin sheets, alloys with many other metals, can be melted and cast into highly detailed shapes, has a wonderful color and a brilliant luster. Gold is a memorable metal that occupies a special place in the human mind.

"Throughout the history of our planet almost every established culture has used gold to symbolize power, beauty, purity and accomplishment. Today we continue to use gold for our most significant objects: wedding rings, Olympic medals, Oscars, Grammys, money, crucifixes and ecclesiastical art. No other substance of the same rarity holds a more visible and prominent place in our society." [2]

Then I saw that God had directed me, and the spiritual aspect of the metaphor of gold became clear. The reason God wanted the word "gold" in the book's title was because of all the people in this world, no one is more useful than an effective Christian.

Christians can engage with all people, no matter the race, color, age, gender, or religious views. They shine with the wonderful, brilliant light of Christ going into all the places in the world: places of employment, businesses, neighborhoods, schools, parks, recreational areas, golf courses, concerts, airports, prisons, everywhere.

---

[1] Otto Scott, writing for *USA Gold.* http://www.scottfreeclinic.org/2015/08/31/if-you-thought-gold-was-precious-check-this-out/

[2] Geology.com http://www.scottfreeclinic.org/2015/08/31/if-you-thought-gold-was-precious-check-this-out/

Christians occupy a special place in the heart and mind of God. From the beginning of time, God established the plan for those who believed in His Son Jesus to obtain power, beauty, purity, and righteousness in Him no matter what their story, no matter what their background. Christianity is unlike any other world religion because of Jesus. No other world religion holds a more visible and prominent place in our society.

Then I began thinking more about the athletic analogies, and the Olympic Games came to mind. When you think about the Olympian athletes you remember how hard these young people work to develop their bodies and sharpen their skills, competing against the best of the best on the world stage.

They start out really young in their particular specialty of athletic ability. They work out constantly, and their moms and dads and families get involved, taking them to practices for years, investing quality time as these athletes prepare for the Olympic Games. When they're ready, they compete in meets and contests, ascending through regional and national competitions until they are ready to be challenged by athletes from other nations, all competing to be the best athlete in the world in their category. Then, they will earn the gold, or the silver, or the bronze. All three of these medals, made of different minerals, are worthy to be on that international platform. It took painstaking time and effort, energy and persistence, consistency, and all the qualities that we as Christian believers also need to exemplify with our work in the world.

It takes time and it takes effort, it takes perseverance, it takes the right people around you, encouraging you, it takes increasing your awareness, your abilities, your understanding as a believer, all of these things to be a Saint of Gold.

So what is **SAINTSOFGOLD** about?

SAINTSOFGOLD is presented as an invitation…an invitation to you to become an Olympian of Christ, a Gold Medal Champion of Faith, a Supreme Spiritual Athlete, a model of the highest level of Christian spiritual performance.

Because you are reading this book, you already have interest in being a Saint of Gold…you are already a Saint of some degree. Now you have the opportunity to learn more about how you can become even more visible as a kind, caring and loving soul, how you can more freely express your qualities of compassion and service, and rise to become a Saint of Gold, furthering God's work during your lifetime.

Now is the time to demonstrate more of the Gold qualities we have as people who claim we are God's Saints. It's time now to move into action!

What will you do today to bring God's love and grace into someone's life? Who do you know who needs a helping hand? How will you remind someone that God is in their life? What small favor can you perform that will mean something precious to another?

Sometimes it's just a smile and a kind word. Sometimes it's bringing some food to a neighbor's house. It could be as simple as picking up somebody's mail for them, or running an errand since you're going in the same direction. Sometimes it's listening to someone tell why they are feeling sad, or taking time to read the Bible together and share a favorite passage.

Our society is so fast-paced and it's so easy to become insulated, many people are left alone and lonely. People aren't hugged during the week, let alone the day, or given gratitude and appreciation from those who live in the very same household. You never know when a smile and a kind word will make all the difference in a person's life. I've felt a person's gratitude many times by doing just this one simple act of service. You have, too!

When you see an ambulance racing by, are you irritated by the shrieking siren or do you think instead that it could be one of your spiritual brothers or sisters in trouble, or someone without God's knowledge and truth, and they're on their way to bring help? Our thought should be for God to send provisions of comfort and care.

Part of being a Saint of Gold is having more awareness about what's happening around us, and showing that we care. Most people don't ever seem to notice anything outside their own intimate family and a few so-called friends.

When we are at work doing our jobs, are we even noticing that our co-workers are hurting? Do we even care if they are? Are we in competition with them? Are we jealous of them? Do we want them to succeed or do we really want them to be defeated in their efforts? Are we happy when they are successful? What kind of selfish and harmful attitudes do we carry with us every day? Is this what a Saint of Gold would do? Of course not.

I am constantly examining myself, trying to be conscious at all times, working at being aware of how I treat other people and how I treat myself. Sometimes I don't like what I see when I look at myself. When I reflect and see something I could've done better, I don't like how I feel. Sometimes I tell myself and God, "Wow, Lord. Is this hard or what?"

It is hard. Going for the gold…that's a hard deal. You have to work at being conscious all the time, guarding yourself against making slips that can hurt somebody or hurt yourself. You have to work at it so much that your very nature changes and you become someone who is strong and positive, not weak and negative. To be a Saint of Gold you're going to have to put in a lot of effort and time! It is definitely intentional.

In our society there is competition in everything we do. We're always competing against each other, but that's wrong. The only competition in which we should engage is competing against our own ability to be a 24 karat gold example. The gold evaluation system is composed of 24 parts, or karats, and the purest form of gold is 24 karats.

The question then becomes, "Which level of purity are you as a Saint of Gold?" Are you a 14 karat gold Saint, an 18 karat gold Saint or 24 karat gold Saint? What's wrong with being a 10 or a 12? What difference does that make? You're still gold, right?

Where Are You Going?

As I mentioned, many babies and children are growing up in home environments where parents are not as supportive as they need to be. These children begin asking questions about their purpose in life, their connection to God, and need help with recognizing and understanding healthy options for what they will do in their lives, and who they can look to for good advice.

Parents are not serving their children when they don't intentionally talk about the fundamentals of life. "Why am I here? What is my purpose? Where am I going?" If children don't get this information from their parents, they will get the answers from somebody else that may not represent the principles and biblical perspectives of God.

Maybe your mother, father or your grandparents didn't do a very good job of passing on this kind of information. The fact of the matter is that one day we're all going to die and we're going SOMEwhere, whether you believe that or not. And yes, some people regard this as programming, and frankly it is, but we are all programmed for something anyway, for either good or bad, right? Your programming might as well be good programming.

My observations have revealed to me that most people seem drawn to the negative, and that may be a function of their family environment, a lack of academic education, submission to accepting bad experiences as a predominant norm, difficulty with health issues, dissatisfaction with unrealized expectations, the loss of dreams for a better life, the association with people who have negative attitudes, and being afflicted with an overbearing addiction like alcohol, drugs, food, gambling, sex, shopping, and the absorption of the constant onslaught of the media's incessant Madison Avenue consumption messages, steady diet of negative news, and low-brow programming.

Now, certainly, I'm no psychologist or human behaviorist, but when I think about these things, I remember the ideas I was taught when my parents were helping me build a strong biblical foundation of understanding.

How can things just come into existence without there being a Creator or Someone who made all of this? I see and understand the science of things, but science doesn't explain the most important part of life, which is, "Why am I here?", "Where am I going?", and "What is my purpose?"

If you have children, it's important to have these kinds of conversations with them so they can develop their inquisitive nature of thinking, expand their understanding, and see the connection between their lives and God.

As recently as 200 years ago, there weren't any or many schools where children could go to learn. Instead, their parents taught them with a home education. That's why today's home school movement is so popular, because parents recognize that the schools are neglecting discussions about the Bible and the values the Bible conveys.

The blessings our society can receive when people are in touch with their spiritual origins are wonderful. For me, it's a blessing when I can be around another believer. Even though that person's background and life experiences may not be like mine, I feel strongly connected to them because they have crossed-over into a different realm of spiritual awareness of who they are. I get excited about that!

The promise of their further development creates expectations for the increased value of who they are now and who they will become. They value themselves, they begin to love themselves and appreciate who they are regardless of their size, shape, or color. They have welcomed spiritual increase into their lives and they are open to the continual blessings that come from this. They are open to receiving the love of the only true God.

To answer the question, "Where are you going?" the answer is one that only you can determine. Are you going down the path of the Lord Jesus, cleansing and purifying yourself as you help others do the same, or are you getting sidetracked, going through a labyrinth of misleading paths that either waste the time of your life or, worse yet, sully your soul's light with the devil's work?

Road Map

Everybody knows the best way to get to a destination is to use a road map or nowadays the GPS. However, the GPS or a road map does not guarantee good parenting destinations, but if the parents don't have some kind of plan of purpose for their children, the child's journey will begin with no sense of direction because the lack of the parents' direction. Both become confused and unsure even in their own community. Road signs and alternate routes all become distracting because the destination was not planned ahead of time.

In fact, it is difficult to find road maps to buy. Technology guides us with Google maps and MapQuest. The modern tech map is very different from the paper maps we used 30 years ago. The roads have changed a lot, with new freeways, all kinds of exciting off-ramps, and a lot of new roads leading in unfamiliar directions. The maps used now, modern navigation satellite systems, are coordinated to all the ills of modern society, and Johnny's new mobile device is telling him to take the shortest path; everybody's driving the new shortest path, and this path leads to a destination that is different and exciting but perhaps toward a dead-end road, a world that has lost its way.

The outer appearances of our lives in this new world have changed tremendously in the last 30 years. Almost everybody has a computer, and even more of everybody has a cell phone. When the cell phones came out they were big, bulky, and had limited ability compared to what they can do now. Today the Internet is in the palm of most everyone's hands and you can find out the weather in Tokyo, watch videos of the Fourth of July fireworks on the top of the Space Needle in April, or read today's news from Rio de Janeiro.

The truth is that we don't need all this additional information and all these technological devices to interact relationally with people. These are all devices that actually keep us separate from each other, keep us from interacting with each other Old School.

The appearance of increased communication between each other is an illusion as we become more and more separated from each other. A television or computer screen in every room of the house usually translates into our living more disconnected lives, not lives of more interconnectivity.

Technology has invaded almost every aspect of our lives, and more and more of these "toys" or "tools" are coming every year. Now we have security cameras watching our front doors and windows. We can turn on lights and raise or lower the thermostat when we're not home. The technology invasion will keep on increasing. Already there are cars that can parallel park themselves. All of these fun inventions would be great if they didn't make us less and less in touch with the natural world and with each other and most importantly, didn't insulate us from our connection with God.

Who's caring about this? We should all be caring! But are we deceiving ourselves in pretending we care? We're not concerned. We're not even fully aware of the impact technology is having on our relationships with each other, or if we are, then only slightly as our 7-second attention span reminds us to change the channel on our TV sets.

The devil, Satan, goes around like a roaring lion seeking who he may devour, and who is he trying to devour? He's trying to devour the people of God, the Saints. If he devours me or you, then that's one less Christian he has to deal with and one more non-believer he possesses.

There are only two destinations: heaven and hell, but if you don't believe that because you didn't get this knowledge as a kid and you strayed as an adult, when you do "get it", the Spirit of the Lord tells you, "Yes, this is real." It is very real.

What is your destination? Well, if you're a believer, you want the destination to be Godly. If you're not a believer, if you're halfway in, halfway out, lukewarm, cold, your destination is different. If you want what the world has, if you want to look like those of the world, if you want to buy what they buy and drive what they drive, then yes, all of that's fantastic…but is there a balance in your life or are you so engaged with the ephemeral that you're losing sight of the Real Deal?

Are you buying Fool's Gold and abandoning the Real Thing?

Too Many Choices

One of the things that's unique about our culture today is the vast amount of choices we have, in every aspect of our daily lives. Take, for example, the question, "What do you want for breakfast?" When I was growing up you had a choice of the cold cereals, Kellogg's cornflakes or Cheerios, or the hot cereals, oatmeal or cream of wheat. Which one do you want? Today you have a choice of 30 or 40 different breakfast cereals! When you go to the store to buy a can of beans you have to pick between 20 different kinds! When I was a kid, there was Heinz beans, or Del Monte beans.

So today, when it comes to choosing a path to walk, a spiritual path, once again there are more choices than there used to be, and some of these choices appear to be healthy but are not authentic spiritual paths or practices. Doing tai chi as a form of meditation might work, but it doesn't bring you into God's house. Practicing yoga is good for the body and the spine, but does it develop your spirit and get you closer to God's Kingdom, while practicing a divine conscientiousness of meditative self individualism? Just because things are good doesn't mean it's good for us.

How does practicing Buddhism or wrestling with Zen koans make you a better Christian? I believe there is too much distraction and too many choices, and they dilute our attention span, leading us further and further away from our Christian faith. We are not to conform to the world but want the world to conform to the things of God. Follow me as I follow who?

Proper and Improper Influences

There are also a lot of daily influences that need to be recognized and dismissed. As I've mentioned, the media is a huge influence with promoting a materialistic and worldly view. The media's goal is to make money through advertising, and they will do whatever will keep you harnessed to their news, weather, comedy, drama, movies, or documentaries. "Don't touch that dial! We'll be right back!"

The only influence in your life should be God because that's where the gold is, that's where our life as servants of God are centered. How do you get this influence? It's available from many sources. You can find it under the roof of a humble church, you can find it in the heart of an honest Christian, you can read about it in the Bible. Your faith will grow as you allow yourself to hear and see God's works, and by reading the Word of God. Your faith in God will grow as you turn away from the noise of this world and filter out the chaos that's dancing dizzily around you, trying in every moment to distract and influence you away from the Truth and the universal truth of Love that is ours.

Failure to Plan and Failure to Follow the Plan

The failure to plan can come from procrastinating to make a plan, or changing your plan and never making headway, and it can come from a stubborn mindset or any variety of dismissive attitudes.

Failing to plan is also a burden of the Saints for not being godly examples, demonstrating and communicating Biblical truths for the younger generations. The Bible says that evil men and imposters will increase in number and grow worse, having more success with deceiving us.

Saints have always played an important role in a disinterested culture rebelling against the Truth of God. Remember, we too were once disinterested and rebellious toward the Word of God. Now we are Saints, ambassadors for a positive change, and people look to us, but when we're not representing our faith properly, we look like liars and cheats and actually behave in these manners. In our hearts we want to represent God well and because we are ambassadors we have a responsibility to look at ourselves and see if we're being rebellious and disobedient, and honest with ourselves. We need to ask ourselves if we are truly being a godly man, woman or child. How many of us really understand what this means?

There are wannabe men and women of God who have become contaminated with the things of this world, and their lives are not flowing in righteousness and godliness, affection, virtue, love, and Truth.

As a Saint of Gold, do you really examine yourself? Are you honest with yourself and going through that transformational process, purifying yourself, moving yourself from a hard piece of granite to a pliable nugget of gold? Who wouldn't want to go through this process? What piece of granite who wants to be gold would speak out and say, "Don't make me gold!" This would be failure, changing the plan and succumbing to your stubbornness, your mindset, your attitude.

The way to move from granite to gold is to hear the unwelcome message that stings you to your core, that tells you are not yet on the right path, that you are deluding yourself with the mistaken belief that you are a good Christian, a Saint of Gold.

Don't get me wrong. You can be a good person, but it takes extra commitment to be a good Christian, and even more conviction and effort to become a Saint of Gold. Even then, it takes more dedication and more exertion of your free will to become a 24 karat Saint of Gold. How about that - let's really go for the gold!

No one said the way would be easy, and those that think it is are fooling themselves all too often, but you can get there. We are all destined to get there, but it will take honest effort and sincere dedication to purify yourself in thought, word, and deed. The first step in becoming a true Saint of Gold is to show kindness and love to yourself. This is how you will receive your strength. You have to be willing to take a spoonful of that nasty castor oil because you know it's going to help you, and after you swallow it down could have a glass of cool and refreshing fruit juice.

Aside from failing to plan, or procrastinating with following through on your plan, some people continually change their plan and slow their progress to a snail's pace.

Sometimes it's a matter of stubbornness and pride. People are born with a variety of traits and temperaments, but all their reluctance, self-justification, excuses and reasoning can be changed when we're born again in Christ.

The purpose of the Saints of Gold Program is to help Saints become better and do God's Will in ever-improving ways. We know we're not perfect, but we are always seeking to glorify God and God's Word. God will help us so we can do this.

People get in a rut sometimes because they've experienced so many negative challenges that influence their mindset and attitude. Disappointment sometimes results in stubbornness against making positive changes and yes, fearfulness of yet another failure. It may be based on cynicism, believing that things will never change, and it may be based on a pattern born of many years of ego-centered struggle.

Sometimes people are hurt so deeply they are unable to break free of the suffering that holds them a prisoner. A person's mindset can get stuck on "I'm hurting, I'm in pain. No one understands. I wish somebody else could feel the pain I have!"

Remember that as a person thinks, so they behave. It's all about your mindset and your attitude. If you're always thinking negative thoughts, that's pretty much how you're going to be feeling, and these feelings will spill over into how you perceive the world is treating you. My dad use to say to me when I was feeling the pains of life, "Daughter, you will never feel the pains of life like Jesus." In other words, the things we go through in life are pale in comparison to what Jesus went through for our life.

It doesn't have to be this way because you have a choice. When you remember your faith in the grace of God, you can change your perception and be on the Lord's side with Christ's mind. We know that Jesus didn't have a negative attitude because He wanted us to think on things that are good, lovely, and pure.

This is the practice we need every day, throughout our day. We need to be around people with good attitudes who can adjust our mindset by their example, helping us with our attitude, reminding us to strengthen our attitudes and remember that we live in God's love. This is how people grow to become better and more equipped in our walk with God.

God offers us His love but what do we do with this love? How are we manifesting it in our lives to help build up the Kingdom; to help people want what we say we have?

PRAYER:

> *Father in Heaven, it is through Your son Jesus that every knee shall bow and every tongue confess His Lordship. Thank you that the Saints know and believe and pray that others, too, will know and believe that Jesus is the way, the truth and the life. No one comes to the Father except through Jesus. He is Immanuel. God with us. As we take a closer look at You through Your word, help the Saints of Gold to really see there is so much more to this life in the giving*

of our lives for others, just as Your Son gave his life for all. I pray that we stop looking at the world for solutions and guidance and look to Jesus, the author and finisher of our salvation.

In Jesus' Name I pray.

Chapter 3

Where Have You Dropped Off Your Faith?

As a Christian, I have to look within and ask myself, "Why do I drop off my faith somewhere, sometimes? I don't want people to think I have all the answers because the truth is I don't, and no one can have all the answers but God. He wills us with His Spirit to do what we need to do and to say what we need to say, and then to give Him some credit for it, like, "Hey, Annette, can I have a little credit for that?"

We walk by faith. We live by faith. Our entire being is through faith in Him. Without faith it's impossible to please God. If you drop faith off, hurry back and pick it up!

The first thing to determine is how do we know that you or I or someone we know has dropped off their faith? It's by hearing how we or they talk. Their diminished faith will be evident in their attitude, mindset, or stubbornness and pride. For example, someone might say to me, "Yes, Annette, you are absolutely right, but---" Wait a minute! There are no buts! You're about to drop off your faith.

As a Saint of Gold, you have to know that God's hand is always in your life, and no matter what your circumstances, there are no buts. When someone forgets their faith, and reverts to their smaller self, you can remind them gently that they are a child of God and a Christian, and ask them to accept their situation as evidence of God's Will in their life. If you have to, because they insist on arguing, you can say silently or aloud, "Satan, in the name of Jesus, I command you to be quiet." I've had to tell friends this occasionally. I realize life can be hard and there can be much pain, sorrow and suffering, debilitating us from expressing our faith and showing a lack of faith; complaining, whining, murmuring without the least gratitude or appreciation of any good in life at length should be addressed with one another.

Sometimes you may need to stay away from people in this condition for awhile because they are so desperate and unwilling to listen. We are God's representation and when we are not whole and healthy, we can make others sick, too. Our focus on our own anxieties disables us from giving goodness to anyone.

"Where have you dropped your faith, Honey?" I ask that a lot. "Where's your faith? It's impossible to please God without it. It's like when your child is not obedient and they don't please you. "You haven't done anything I've asked you to do, nothing!" I'd tell others. "And you're not showing any gratitude or faithfulness about anything." Sometimes you just have to distance yourself from people who are so committed to being in pain, so unwilling to find their faith as their best way for going through a terribly hard time.

Your relationship with your family is critically important, of course. When I was growing up we had family time, usually at dinner, because that's when our family would come together. We would talk about our day and share our experiences and observations. Many families these days don't have any real family time, at dinner or any other time. It's very hard to build family relationships when you're always on the go. You're in the car, you're at a basketball or football game, your children are active and need to balance their social and school time, and building relationships can suffer. Even with one spouse working and one spouse taking care of the home and children, our family social time has become more hit-and-miss.

As a Saint of Gold, you have to examine your relationships, and the most primary relationship is your relationship with God. If your relationship with God is not so good, it's probably not so good with your family, either. You might think your family relationships are strong, but when the storm comes, that's when you'll really know. The 21st century children of Israel, the Saints of Gold, are wandering in the wilderness of our society, living in the promised land of good and plenty and service and love toward one another.

The saints are murmuring and complaining, we want all the things that the rest of the culture has, the nice cars, the nice homes, the nice vacations, furnishings, clothes, all the things, and are being deceived and distracted by the messages of this materialistic and weakened spiritual culture.

The other day I heard someone refer to their spouse as their "partner". I don't like that word for a husband-wife situation. You hear it in the media a lot, and because of this, lots of people are using it in their own daily language. When we use the "partner" word, we are changing the dynamics of our immediate family. After our relationship with God, the next important relationship is our relationship with our immediate family, and it's disturbing to notice that the influences that are all around us are affecting our family and our relationship with our brothers and sisters and the rest of our family. The influences of our social system are undermining the dynamics within our families.

A workman came to do some work on my house and for some reason he was talking about the homosexual movement. When he was speaking with me, he said, "My partner…" and I said, without thinking about it, "Are you gay?"

He said," Oh, my God! No! What made you say that?"

I replied, "I'm sorry. I said that because you said the word 'partner'."

He said, "No, I'm a Christian and I've been married to my wife for 30+ years."

When we change our wording and our language, we also change the structure and content of our thoughts, which also affects our feelings. The system we live in changed all the spousal wording about 25 years ago. I remember because I was working for the state government at the time, and gradually this wording became ingrained in the system and eventually in our standard vocabulary.

The "partner" word always confuses me because I don't know if the person is gay, or referring to their wife, husband, or business partner.

Being politically correct has made many of us afraid to speak 'our' truths. This is especially true in the work environment. My last job was very difficult. I worked for a private company owned by a family. The company needed to hire someone and applicants were interviewed by my supervisor who was also the CEO. I helped with the interview process, and one candidate in particular seemed to have the skills the company needed.

I was surprised when my boss asked me," Are you going to be okay working with him?"

I responded with surprise. "What do you mean, will I be okay?"

"Well, I guess you didn't recognize his gender preference. My guess is he's a homosexual."

"Really?" I said. "I didn't know that. Of course I can work with him. The question is, rather, will he be okay working with me?"

The man was hired and we worked together very well for the first few months. When he first began working, he made it very clear to me that he had a partner. I also made it very clear to him that I'm a child of God and I believe what the Bible says.

The first two years were hell.

My boss didn't know how to handle either one of us. As it should be, as a Saint of gold, I was always the one with the forgiving heart, and a forgiving attitude. I was the one with the right mindset. I wasn't stubborn about trying to make things work. We were in a working environment, and we had to do our best to get along because there were projects and assignments we had to complete. It's okay to talk and be in the light of the Spirit. We don't have to be afraid to have conversations and hide and disguise our faith.

It's okay for other people to have ideologies, persuasions, and perspectives. And it's okay for me to have mine, too. Our beliefs happen to not agree with each other, so we can agree to disagree and still work together, still love one another and be cordial and civilized to each other.

I told him, "That's all fine. I still love you. I'm not offended. I have a compassionate heart for you. I will pray that God will help to change your intolerance and bigotry toward me, and therefore toward God."

Can we find a way to do this? Can we just all get along? Especially in the body of Christ, can we do this as a church? If we can't do this as a church, how effective are we going to be outside the church? The purpose of the church is to equip us with understanding and knowledge, and increase our awareness as a spiritual being, as the spiritual essence that's within me.

If not, then my struggle is harder because I don't have the love I need from my brothers and sisters, and my work is more difficult with people outside the church body who are not claiming God, who are not claiming Christ as their Savior.

The main point is that we need to look closely at our relationships and do our best to walk with God in these relationships with others, especially with family, work, church, and friends.

You can be strong in yourself, strong in God, strong in Jesus, and from that level of faith where your relationships are the strongest, be tolerant, accepting, and live your faith in every deed, and in every word, and with everyone you meet.

Bringing Others Along

I believe God puts people in our lives for a reason, and they're either bringing us along or we're bringing them along, bringing us or them along toward a higher quality of life that serves God and Christ.

Salt and light. That's what we are, we're the salt. When I think of salt, I think of it as cleansing, and as a preservative. I also think of salt as a seasoning that brings out the flavor in food. Like salt, Christians bring more flavors to the pot and season the relationships, starting with me, and starting with you. I am salt, just like you.

We are also a light. You can be in the darkest of rooms, and even in very large rooms with just one tiny match, people are able to see the light. This is how we are, Christians are light, in our society today. If too dim a light, it can still be seen, though vaguely. It's dark all around us and there is not enough light, except when we show our light and bring others along, our light shines brighter and more people are automatically attracted to us.

People around us are hungry to know the Truth, are waiting for someone to show them the way, to help them find sanctuary and wholesomeness, and a respite from the storms of their life, looking for a way to be peaceful, reassured, loved. When people see your light as a Saint of Gold, they will be drawn to you, seeking out the light you carry so they also can walk a path of peace and purpose.

When we develop our light and it's attractive enough to draw others, people will automatically come. People automatically came to Jesus because wherever He went He was a light, healing and delivering, and people are drawn to this. They are. And when they're drawn to us these days, what are we giving them? Do we give them anything of real substance? Do we give them the gospel? We should give them something that serves their spirit, right?

As Saints of Gold, we need to learn not to judge people, particularly one another. A lot of times we judge how they come to us or why they're coming to us. We may not actually verbalize anything that we're thinking, but we're automatically judging, analyzing, and assessing, trying to figure out the person from their appearance, from what they're saying, what they're driving, where they live, their abilities and intellect. We have a strong tendency to prejudge, and while we may be judging the sinner, we find ourselves doing what the sinner does. We are not here to judge others. We are only here to serve God, to love and serve others and to spread the good news of the Truth of the Bible.

It's not our place to judge others by how they look or what they say because we don't know where they are in their walk with Christ until we start having relationships with these people who are coming to us. Once we start a relationship with them we can then begin to talk and season everything with grace and love. (There's that salt seasoning again, flavoring the food and bringing out the quality of the ingredients.)

We can exercise control over our mind, we can shut down that harsh thinking and that cruel judgment and instead embrace that person, bring them in, find out about them, let our light shine so they see a way out of the darkness. We can throw some of our seasoning on them and then let God do what He does. Talk about the gospel, remember that. Talk about the Word of God. Remember that it's Alive and Powerful. Let's not just go out to lunch and as believers never mentioned God or Jesus, never mention anything spiritual. We are different, so BE DIFFERENT!

I go out and I've talked with my friends about Jesus and God's love for us, and it's been just great! Several times people within earshot have come by our table and said, "Wow, thank you. We heard your conversation. It was wonderful. Thank you." Many people are eager to exchange their loss for fulfillment, and use your light to light their own. But if we never talk about God and Jesus and the gospel, how can anyone ever find us in the darkness?

We can control our minds. We have authority over our thoughts and actions, and we can choose whether to allow our thoughts to move us into positive or negative actions. We have to ask ourselves, which choice is predominantly controlling our lives? Which one are you, Saint? Are you controlling your mind and your behavior, Saint?

This is what I see. Are you seeing it, too? Maybe others are seeing it but those believers aren't saying anything. The nonbelievers are definitely talking about it, whatever 'it' is for the world, leading more people into temptation, but I don't hear a lot of Christians talking about the importance of making good choices, following the Christian path, showing others by their example how God through Jesus have asked us to live, and to love and respect each other first.

Saints of Gold need to be more bold, need to ask more questions and communicate, and bury whatever fear you feel in the strength and power of your faith. We need to have more transparent communication; we need to find a way to tell the people we meet about the importance of making good choices, shining our light, and showing the way through the teachings of the gospel.

But the saints of today complain and whine and say, "That's not my thing. I can't do that. It's not my place to say something. What are people going to say?"

My response is, "Come on! We need to set a higher standard. God wants us to set a higher standard, and you need to step up!" Yes, we are different, but not in a strange way. We are unique. The system, society, has made us strange and over time has made us feel ineffectual and outnumbered. I am different, and you are different, too. It doesn't bother me. I'm not offended by being different. I'm not concerned because I am in God's hands. My faith is strong.

I have earned the right to speak because I have practiced, I have listened, I have participated. I have read, and I have prayed to God to help me. I speak the values and beliefs of God. That's what I do and I'm not ashamed of that anymore. I'm not even ashamed that I was once ashamed!

Many years ago I worked at a university; I was a student there at the same time. As a matter of fact, they allowed me to be a full-time student as I worked full time. One day I got a letter. "Congratulations! You are on the Dean's List." Working hard, being diligent, persevering, doing good work and having a spirit of excellence pays off, and that's what I did.

The next thing I knew, they were trying to get rid of me because the enemy wanted me to go before I completed my degree because I was salt and light. They really mistreated me, to get me to let go. The Lord has said that we will be persecuted for His name's sake. Well, they knew what I represented; they knew who I was.... and God said, "No, you are here to get your degree, and you tell them that."

So I told them that. I said, "You cannot let me go right now. There's no reason why I should go and not complete my degree here, which they paid for, mind you. There is no reason for that, and in spite of the hurt you give me, I still respect your authority and positions, and still have love toward you, looking beyond your mistreatment toward me. But I'm not going until I satisfy God's Will for me here." Where did I get that courage and boldness as salt and light?

I did not give in to them. I was not afraid to stand up. I was not a closet saint. I was out of the closet. I stood firmly in God's light for me. I finished my degree, and with honors. Only then was my assignment complete to leave the university, after I satisfied God's purpose.

PRAYER:

> *Father in heaven, the great I AM. It is not Your will that anyone should perish and that all should come to the saving grace and knowledge of Your Son Jesus. It is by faith that we do this. I pray that Saints have genuine faith, uplifting faith and encouraging faith. Thank you for giving us the Holy Spirit to teach us and help us to walk in our faith, the faith of the cross and His blood for the redemption of our sins. I pray that we regularly examine our relationship with You first to keep us in fellowship with You, which helps build better relationships with others. We can do nothing without You, Father. You are our Shepherd and we do not have to want.*
>
> *In Jesus' Name I pray.*

Chapter 4

Let the Saints Come Out of the Closet

It's time now for the Saints to come out of the closet. For years, even decades, we have seen all types of people proclaiming themselves and their group, and they are no longer ashamed, no longer hidden, no longer afraid, and willing to stand up for their beliefs and who they are.

We've seen the LGBTQ community come out of the closet, the Wiccans, Satanists, Black Lives Matter, White Power, Antifa, and all kinds of groups come out of the closet and demand to be recognized and heard.

It's time now for Christians to do the same thing, don't you think? Why shouldn't we also come out of the closet to proclaim and profess that we are believers in Christ? We believe in His death, burial and resurrection. We believe in the Bible. We believe that Christ is the Son of God. We believe that Christ is returning. We believe in righteousness and sin. We believe in all of this and we shouldn't have to be afraid to state our position and our beliefs.

Somewhere along the line we lost our willingness to proclaim our faith. We became mesmerized by the culture we live in, we were browbeaten into keeping quiet and living invisibly. We came to accept the social behaviors of being polite and keeping quiet, not talking about how important God and Jesus are in our lives and for the spiritual development and health of the people in our country and around the world. We have let ourselves down as Saints, choosing to be hermits in the closet rather than proclaimers in the Light.

Don't get me wrong! I'm not saying we have to be impolite, but I am saying we should have no hesitation speaking our Truth when the moment is right, when our knowledge and our understanding of spiritual wisdom can help somebody in need. We have a living, powerful, real message. We have knowledge of the Word of God! We can be a force of strength and compassion, reassurance and direction in our communities, with the people we meet in our daily walk with God. I believe the time of silence is over and we need to become more visible and proactive as Saints of Gold.

The world is coming out, but they are coming out against their own consciousness. They are coming out and standing for something that's untruthful and displeasing to God, and we can no longer be afraid, unwilling, or too defeated to speak up and speak out. We are of God, we believe in Christ, we believe in His death and resurrection, we believe in the Bible. The world, with its societal ills and abnormalities, needs to hear our message, too, the message of the Word of God. How can we keep silent any longer? How can you keep silent?

The truth is we shouldn't, and this is why sermons are a must. What is a sermon? A sermon is a talk about a religious or moral topic based on a passage in the Bible. If we are going to be Saints of Gold and not Saints of Tin or Saints of Aluminum, we have the right and the responsibility to talk about morality and authentic Christian behavior for the guidance and improvement of those who are present.

Sermons can be given by anybody, including by you and by me. Sermons should be about the gospel, the good news, the message of hope, and anyone who speaks the truth about God and Jesus can give a sermon. You don't have to be an ordained minister or theologian to talk about Jesus's salvation and hope for us as individuals. People tend to think of a sermon as theologically scripted but to me a sermon is a message of the gospel. Every Saint of Gold has a sermon to give to open ears and hearts.

Because all of us are sinners, Saints of Gold may be unwilling to come out of the closet and speak the Truth. Some Saints of Gold may mistakenly believe they are poor examples because the events in their life have been so horrible they have lost the right to speak out. Saints of Gold have had premarital sex, adulteries, abortions, divorces, have stolen, lied, cheated and killed…but no matter what past mistakes, loss of control, or debauchery has expressed itself in our life, once you have accepted Christ, you are forgiven your sins and can step out of the darkness of the closet. You have the right and obligation to speak to those who will listen so they can know the love and grace of God.

Your past mistakes will not be forgotten, that's true, and they will follow you, but now they are no longer a weight to hold you back. People may talk and point their fingers, but once you've taken Jesus as your Savior, their darkness can no longer hurt you. As a Saint of Gold your duty is to move on and carry your Truth to those who need to hear it.

We are all in the same boat. We have all fallen short, and we are all sinners, but God is cleaning us up and making us whole, making us better through this journey of sanctification…which is what your life and walk with God is all about.

When we're not honest with ourselves, we stay hidden. We can't come out as openly because we are concealing something and so our voice is diminished, our truth is slighted. The world certainly comes out, open and unashamed of their lifestyles, and these people show no consciousness of being responsible to God. This is why we, as Saints of Gold, who are aware of our responsibilities to God, also need to become visible and in spite of our past mistakes.

I believe that as the Saints of Gold come out of the closet and begin delivering sermons about the good news, we will find many people with receptive hearts because God is always drawing every one of us to Him. Of course we can't understand Him. His ways are higher than ours, His thoughts are higher than our thoughts, and I think sometimes that because we can't understand as much as we want, we focus on that, which keeps us in the closet instead of focusing on the Truth and delivering the Word of God.

There has to be a balance in all things, of course. You have to look at yourself first. First seek the Kingdom of God and demonstrate righteous behavior. When you do this, the way for you will be opened even more.

Being a Saint of Gold also means being an evangelist, spreading the Christian gospel through preaching or through your own personal witness. Saints are called to do so, to go and make disciples. What is a disciple? A disciple is a follower and believer of Christ. We have an obligation to tell people the gospel, the good news, and let them know about the hope that lies within you.

Many people who call themselves Christians don't feel the hope they have been told about and given. If you don't have any hope, it's hard to tell someone else about it. If you're always feeling downtrodden and heavy with negativity, you're probably not feeling good about your relationship with Christ.

As a disciple of Christ, how can you not feel hopeful? No matter what storms are passing through your life, your primary relationship is with God and you know your earthly existence is merely a passage of time and events, and no hardship, no difficulty, no insult or loss can ever overcome your knowing that God is always with you, protecting you and loving you. Your sanctuary is with God, so how can you not feel hope?

Christians who whine and complain, who spread their negativity and hopelessness have forgotten the gift they received when they accepted Christ as their Savior. Yes, it's true that some Saints may be afflicted with medical conditions and medicines that might tilt the apple cart, but most Saints who talk endlessly about their problems are forgetful of the blessings they have received through the grace of God.

Saints of Gold remember that we have a super-natural strength inside us, which is the Holy Spirit, and when we call on Him, He will comfort us. This is the promise that was made, and he is always available to us in the midst of any storm. It doesn't matter if the storm is a spring rain or a Cat-5 hurricane, God is always present in our life. Remember this when something difficult occurs. Call for support and guidance from God and you will receive it.

Some Christians will say, "It hurts too much! I don't want to hear it! Tell someone else the good news!" and they will be moaning and groaning and complaining and never think to call on Jesus. Saints of Gold know they are an example in their time of turmoil. We know there are shadows of darkness we'll have to confront in our earthly life, but we also know to reach for the love and grace that is always available.

Evangelism can happen anytime and anywhere. It's not relegated to Sundays at church. I speak about God and His son Jesus, I tell the good news whenever I can. I do this because the good news is always on my mind and in my heart. It is never far away from me, but always present. As a Saint of Gold, my connection with God through Jesus is always in the forefront. Just as some people speak about the weather because it's so evident, so also do I speak about the presence of God in my life. I don't get obnoxious about it, although maybe sometimes I do, but it's not because I'm trying to push my beliefs on others, it's because I'm excited about the Truth I know, about the hope I feel, about the love that's always pouring from my heart. Wow! Please don't hate!

Some people get excited about the weather, or their children, or their dogs, or about their great vacation. Sure, all those things are wonderful, but what can be more wonderful, more evident, more joyous than knowing we are in the heart of God, that our sins are forgiven, that we are loved without end? I truly don't know any greater conversation piece!

Just recently I was speaking with my neighbor. I talk with my neighbors all the time, and there's this very nice man who lives next door. He just returned from a trip to Europe. He saw the castles, the ornate palaces, museums of art, and all the usual things tourists do and see. As he was telling me his experiences and the beauty of it all, a thought came into my mind about how much beauty awaits us who love God. I said to him, "Our eyes have not seen, our ears have not heard, nor entered into hearts, the glorious things of absolute unimaginable beauty and awe that awaits the saint. This is revealed to us by His Spirit."

> "However, as it is written: "What no eye has seen, what no ear has heard, and what no human mind has conceived", the things God has prepared for those who love him—these are the things God has revealed to us by his Spirit." (1 Corinthians 2:9-10)

My neighbor was startled and he said, "You're talking about Heaven?"

I said, "No, I'm talking about here on Earth. I know Heaven's going to be unimaginable as well. We're going to be here on Earth!"

After a moment he got the picture and thought about it, then said, "Yeah, I can see what you're saying."

I was happy I had just evangelized to my neighbor. I find myself doing that to my neighbors. They know me. They see me outside and they come over to talk, and that's when I can do some evangelizing. I don't put myself down if my conversation was weak and watered down or didn't come out right. I get excited that I spoke up about the real meaning of life.

As a Christian and a Saint of Gold, I'm doing, I'm not just talking. I'm doing. I'm putting my faith into action by speaking up God. Faith without work is dead. It's not just about talking. Talk is very cheap. What you need to do as a Saint of Gold is talk UP Jesus (mention your faith in Him) take action for Him, speak; but be careful of your works, they are watching to see if you have truly come out of the closet. Are they pleasing to God?

When do we evangelize? I'm very spontaneous so I guess God says, "Just go for it, Girl!" I feel led all the time to go for it, but there are times when you should and shouldn't. There's a time to do everything, as in Ecclesiastes 3:

> "To everything there is a season,
> and a time to every purpose under the heaven:"

So there is a time to evangelize and speak about Jesus, and a Saint of Gold must be mindful of this. There is a season, there is a time, but some people, as with John the Baptist, are used specially by God just to be a voice in the Wilderness, crying out. Sometimes I feel this way, sometimes I feel very alone on the path that God has me walking. Sometimes I feel this way, but do I shut down? No, I speak up.

I speak up when I see there is a need to convey a message, to right a wrong, to teach, to help another see the inconsistencies between one's beliefs and one's practice. Coming out of the closet means being spiritually involved in every possible way, as much as circumstances appropriately allow.

What level of Saint are you? What level of Saint do you want to be? Do you want to be a Saint of Bronze, or a Saint of Silver? If you want to be a Saint of Gold, do you want to be 14, 18 or 24 karat gold? The more karats there are, the more pure the gold, and Saints of Gold know the rewards of their Sainthood are not on this earth, but in Heaven they are great.

One of the necessary skills of being a Saint is having patience! You've heard the expression, "She has the patience of a saint"? Well, it's true!

Perhaps you've heard the term "The Fruit of the Holy Spirit". This refers to the nine attributes of a person who is living in alignment with the Holy Spirit. It comes from the Epistle to the Galatians, and states:

> "But the fruit of the Spirit is love, joy, peace, patience, kindness, goodness, faithfulness, gentleness, and self-control." (Galatians 5:22)

The one I personally like the most is patience. I have kindness going on, and I've got love, and joy, too, but not enough of any of them if I don't also have patience. I sometimes hear people talk about patience and they say, "Don't ask for patience because God will give it to you and then you'll be doing everything for everybody! People will run right over you like a doormat!" But that's not what patience is all about. Jesus has patience with us, Jesus is willing to listen to us without getting short-tempered.

Do you have any brothers or sisters? I do. I also have lots of cousins, nieces, and nephews, and I've had to learn to be patient! Having patience with people is important. We need to have patience with each other and let people say what they need to say. When you get short on patience, you stop listening and you stop being open, and that leads to undesirable consequences.

It's true, people like to complain, and one of the main reasons is because they don't realize they have good news in Christ. It's like the children of Israel, finally released from Egyptian slavery. They had God right there, a pillar of cloud by day and a pillar of fire by night. God was right there guiding them, but even the patience of Moses was wearing thin because the Israelites were complaining so much.

It's the same thing here in the United States. We complain continuously. We want this and we want that. We don't like him and we don't like her. Why this and not that? I don't want to and you can't make me. However, if I believe and trust in my Father who is in Heaven, and I know He is my keeper, my source, my All…then I should stop whining and do what I'm supposed to do!

When we don't exhibit patience, we separate from our involvement. If we don't have enough patience to stay committed long enough, we won't see the results that can help you, and which then help me. Yes, patience is an inconvenience sometimes, but obeying God, obeying God's intentions for us, is something we have to do. Spiritual involvement takes us places we didn't think we would go for the sake of others, and in doing this, by being patient and supporting others with our presence, we stay spiritually involved for our benefit and theirs.

Stepping Stones

As Saints of Gold, when we emerge from the closet and engage spiritually, there are stepping stones to lead us along our path. Because we've been in the closet so long and our experiences and practices may be tenuous for lack of use, one of the first stepping stones available to us is loving other saints.

These other saints are people around us who are believers like us. They are at different levels of understanding God's Word, at different levels of commitment to being seen out of the closet, different levels of willingness to bond with other saints, to tell the good news, to dedicate their life, energy, and resources to living their life as a Saint. They might be silver or bronze Saints, they might be 10 karat gold Saints. You'll probably find all kinds of different Saints, and that's okay. What's important is that we connect with each other because of our belief in Christ. When we build our local community of Saints, we are fortifying each other and lending strength to our purpose of supporting each other with spreading the good news and improving our own walk with God.

Another important stepping stone is loving our neighbors as our self. Our neighbors are not just the family living across the street or next door, but anyone God puts in our path. Those are our neighbors. There is a reason why God puts these neighbors in our path, and we are meant to greet them and treat them well, be kind and compassionate and show our love as Christians in happy obedience to God's Will. It's easy to forget in the busy swirl of the day that every soul we see is important to God, and as God's representative, it is our responsibility and our joyful obligation to extend God's loving hand and heart.

Then there is also our own family, people who are related to us. It always amazes me when I speak with people who have siblings, and they haven't spoken in years. Their relationship was damaged because of something that happened 50 years ago when they were children, and they never made up. I've seen families, and I'm sure you have too, where children have divorced their mothers and fathers, or mothers and fathers have divorced their children. It's incredible how our hearts and minds can become so cold and uncaring about people in our own blood family.

As Saints of Gold, we need to heal these relationships. Someone has to be the first to reach out and ask for forgiveness. If God can forgive, we should, too; it is a must. When we think and feel and live small, these hurts are as gigantic as the Himalayan Mountains. When we look at these transgressions from God's perspective, they are as tiny as a grain of sand. As Saints of Gold, it is our blessing to see the Big Picture, to have a large and generous heart, to be God's angels here on Earth, and extend the hand of God's love as we step along the path of spiritual involvement.

Another stepping stone is those people who are deemed unlovable. These are souls living a life of earthly debasement. They may be drug dealers or drug addicts, people who are larcenous or licentious, souls that have thrown off all connections to the sacred and holy, choosing an earthly life of indignities. As Saints of Gold, we remember we were once disgraced, too, in the sight of God. No man can be righteous and pure and holy without God, without practicing God's Will on Earth, and as everyone you see is a sinner, yet we are all loved by God. No soul is unlovable to Him, and Saints of Gold know this and reach out with love to those that appear unlovable to earthly eyes.

My dad was good at this. He would pick up drunks and people who smelled bad, and put them in his car and take them somewhere where they could have a safe night's sleep. My dad was always helping people who crossed his path and were struggling. We don't know their story. We don't know about their struggle. We don't know why they have fallen. We don't know about their walk with God. What we do know is that every soul here on Earth is loved by God, and if God loves souls that are in great trouble, then who are we as Saints of Gold to be repelled by them? Every soul has unlimited capacity to become whole again, to be purified and restored, to join the brethren of God's Christian community.

A friend told me a story about a Christian man who was driving his pickup truck home after an errand in town. Driving over a highway bridge, he noticed a man lying in a culvert where he had apparently spent the night. The man was disheveled with old torn clothes, had a dirty beard and hadn't had a shower in a long time. The truck driver pulled over and went down the highway slope to talk to the stranger. The homeless man had lost his job and lost his home, lost his family, and was surviving the best he could. The driver asked him if he wanted to have a meal and get cleaned up, and so the two men went back to the driver's house. The stranger was simply a man who had fallen on hard times, and with the love and kindness of this Christian man, the stranger became restored in body and spirit, and eventually became a martial arts master with his own dojo and students, and dedicated to an honorable Christian life.

The driver of the pickup truck was clearly a Saint of Gold, and he changed a man's life who then changed the lives of others. We can't know why God puts someone in our path, but everyone can always use a smile, a helping hand, words of support, our friendship and love.

Rather than ignoring people, we could instead unknowingly be helping a new Joel Osteen or a new Dr. Martin Luther King, Jr. When we see someone who needs care and compassion, our opinion doesn't matter. We need to step up and just do what needs to be done, and do it as good Christians, as Saints of Gold. I understand that some of this will seem very unpleasant at first, but that's the nature of this gig. Are we Saints or Aints? Are we true Christians, or pretend Christians? Are we going to stay in the darkness and anonymity of the closet, or step forward into the Light? Are we Tin Saints, Bronze Saints, Silver Saints…and if we are Saints of Gold, how far are we willing to go to prove our worth? Are we brave enough to do what we know needs to be done? How are you going to stand before God when it is your time and offer excuses instead of your pure heart?

When we recognize and behave like true Christians, there is no need to apologize about what we say and do. When we act as Saints of Gold, we act with integrity, honor and love. This is who I am, this is who we are. There is no need for an apology. As Christians we do not need to apologize that we believe in the Bible, we love God, we believe in His Son. This is not about who we are as individuals. This is not about me, me, me, I, I, I. This is about God, about the Spirit of the Lord and His Will. "Lord, you put me in this, so tell me what You want me to do. Show me what You want me to do." As true Christians, we cannot let our ego (Everything Going Okay) get in the way of everything going God's way.

Stumbling Blocks

Are there stumbling blocks? Of course. Everyone has them. Some are visible and some are not. I know you've heard the saying, "Be kind, for everyone you meet is fighting a hard battle."

When I was writing this book and preparing the **SAINTSOFGOLD** Program, I was confronted by my own stumbling blocks. One that was hindering me was fear, because I was afraid that my book wouldn't be good. Another stumbling block was doubt as I wondered if this book could help people. Fear and doubt are the biggest challenges for saints and must be dealt with strategically, and by this I mean with God's help.

I know that the enemy, the spirit of anti-Christ, or Satan, or whatever we choose to call him is always trying to minimize us, make us less powerful, make it harder for us to recognize our purpose, make it more difficult to obey the Will of the Lord. He wants us to think we're too old, we're too young, or we don't have enough education, we're not intelligent, we're black, we're white, we're Asian, we have big eyes or small eyes, we have big lips or bad teeth, we're not strong enough, we're this and that and the other thing… On the inside we think were not understood, we don't receive enough love or kindness or forgiveness…

And yet, these are self-inflicted wounds because in the eyes of God we are completely worthy, we are all made in the image of God, and we are all here to meet the mandate of God's Will the best we can just the way we were created.

As Saints of Gold, we must remind ourselves and we must remind those who cross our path that we are all worthy in the eyes of God. We have the promise that God loves us all, and this love is a forever, unending love. We have the promise that one day, by accepting His Son, we will have eternal life with Him. We have the right to stand up for the Truth, and we have the right to believe in our faith.

To overcome the stumbling blocks that appear in our path, we have to be able to take physical action, and that means being exercised, eating the right foods, getting the right amount of sleep, drinking enough water; and doing all of the things that are going to make an impact on our physical presence.

We also have to read our Bible to exercise our knowledge of God's Word. We have to be around other believers to give and receive strength from each other. We have to pray so we can be constantly in touch with our Savior so we can continually perform the service required of us. We have to use our willpower to say "I can!" instead of "I can't…" There's a list of things we have to do to improve our lives, first for ourselves, and then so we can be a positive influence for others. We need to exert effort, intentional effort. Yes, yes, yes, we will be met with challenges, and as Saints of Gold we need to be strong enough to not only overcome the challenges, but to do so as excellent Christian models of God's love and grace.

As Saints of Gold, it is our responsibility to instruct people and inspire them to take positive action in their lives and in the lives of those they influence.

You may already live a good life, and that's wonderful. Yet even though you may always try to do your best, there are still times when you don't do the right thing. Perhaps you get angry when someone gets angry at you. Perhaps you walk past the homeless person on the street corner who's asking for some spare change. Perhaps you know you could contribute more to your church, or your town, or to a youth club attended by your children or your neighbor's children. Whatever it is, you know you can do better. We can all do better!

Now, today, this is your chance to recognize your shortcomings and change your responses the next time you are challenged. You have many opportunities throughout your day to do the right thing, to recognize the incorrect responses you would normally make before they happen and instead become inspired by your faith and God's Love to make the right choice. Instead of turning away from your obligation, you transform into becoming more evidence of God's presence on Earth, of God's presence in your life.

Come out of the closet and become a Saint of Gold!

PRAYER:

> *Father in Heaven, who are we that You are mindful of us? We have forgotten to redeem the time here on earth. Please forgive us. It is now the time not to be ashamed of the gospel of Jesus Christ, because it is the power of God to salvation for everyone who believes, first to the Jews and to everyone. I pray as Saints of Gold we are coming out of the closet, stronger and wiser with the message of hope, healing, joy and peace. Saints are being built-up within to recognize and resist lies, heresies, and untruths by studying your Word and doing Your Word. I pray that the world will begin to take notice of the authority that's been given to Saints because we are a powerful force. We as Saints are taking back what the enemy has stolen from our loved ones, starting with our children. Thank you for Your grace and mercy in doing so.*
>
> *In Jesus' name I pray.*

Chapter 5

False or Fact?

Resources

One of the big issues Christians have to face at this time in the development of our culture is the highly pervasive nature of the media. Not only has the media invaded our daily lives to an extreme degree, but we also have to be circumspect about whether or not the experiences and the information we're receiving is fact or fiction, true or false.

When I use the word "media" I am referring to both the wide variety of technical devices we use every day, as well as the materials we view, listen to or read. On this list are such things as mobile phones, television, laptops and tablets, the cinema, video games, current popular youth-oriented genres of music, and the influence of popular books and magazines that shape human opinion and beliefs.

We have to remember that the primary purpose of these culture-shaping systems is to make a profit, and because of that they are highly suspicious when it comes to gauging the value they represent. Of course, all these tools can be useful if they present an honest and helpful function, but in most cases they feed our lower and less-evolved interests.

For example, take Harry Potter. This has been a very popular book and movie series because of the personable nature of the characters, the compelling drama, and both the pleasurable and frightening emotions the books and movies conjured in children as well as adults. The premise of the stories is the battle between Good and Evil, and that is a battle that is being waged in our own lives, making the stories personal in some ways and deceptively more accepting for the believer.

However, the other element of its premise is the promotion of supernatural powers rather than the reliance on our relationship with God and Jesus. What would've happened if Harry Potter, instead of being a young magician, had instead been a prophet of God? A young disciple, fully cognizant and accepting of the gifts of our Father, and provided the God-bestowed powers to co nfront evil much like Moses with the 10 Plagues of Egypt? As you can see, the story would've had a much different effect, more in line with our beliefs and intentions as Christians.

It seems to me that the question needs to be asked of Christian parents whether or not they should be allowing their children to read or see these materials when the books and movies are contrary to our beliefs as Christians. We have to be careful, not only with educating our children, but also with preventing our own relaxed attitudes toward contradictory influences. Fact or fiction? Truth or fantasy? Where do we draw the line between permitting an enjoyable fantasy or misleading our youth and ourselves about the Truth?

What we allow ourselves and our children to listen to, or see in the movies, or play on computer screens has a strong and meaningful effect on our lives and theirs, and this influence can take us further from our relationship with God because it introduces a separation between what we think and what we do. It may seem simple, but it's actually very serious and dangerous. I believe it's especially dangerous now when our cultural attitudes are so casual; it's very easy now for us to get lost in the gray areas of the relaxed parenting we see so often.

I'm not saying we shouldn't enjoy stories like Harry Potter because they are, after all, entertaining, and we can't expect every story to feature the struggle between God and the devil, but rather I think the bigger issue is that parents don't discuss stories like Harry Potter with their children, don't examine the issues of magic and fantasy and counter them with the truth available in the Bible and the gospel. It's this lack of balance I believe must be corrected, because if we don't teach our children, the media surely will.

Many of you reading this book remember the time when television and media were much less pervasive. I grew up in an era when television was just becoming popular and available in people's homes. There was no television in my house until I was about six or seven years old. My older brothers and sisters weren't subject to the influence of television, but my younger siblings saw television regularly.

Even so, in those days television was very different. The movies and sitcoms were much less violent or abusive when compared to what is on television these days. Certainly there was bias in the television shows, but they were more gentle, too. We used to watch *Father Knows Best*, and *I Love Lucy*. There was *The Dick Van Dyke Show, Sanford and Son*, and *The Jeffersons*. Besides, we weren't allowed to sit around and watch a lot of TV because Mom and Dad had rules. We could only watch a certain amount, and we had to go outside and play.

There were no cell phones in those days… just board games, and we played those as a family. We were sent outside into the fresh air, and we ran around and played Hide and Seek, and ball games, and rode bicycles. The most important part of all this was that we interacted with each other, we played with each other, we learned to socialize with each other, and our interaction was guided by our love and respect for each other…at least most of the time!

Little by little our culture began to change, and because we are a visual society, and possibly because we were trained so well by television, we began to interact with our screens to a degree that now is almost all-encompassing. The media has grabbed hold of our society as never before, and now we live in the Information Age where we rely on the Internet, our cell phones, our laptops, and have become almost dependent on them. I'm sure you've heard the joke about when the power goes out and people can't use their machines at night, a lot of babies are born nine months later. Funny or not, this example points to not only how reliant we are on these technical devices, but how removed we have become in our relationships.

The most important relationship is our relationship with God, and when we are absorbed by these screens, we are less inclined to be aware of and connect with the Truth. We become separated from our Truth. The screen has become our God and the Internet our Bible.

This, to me, and to you as a Saint of Gold, is horrifying. The devil has done his work well, and with our permission. I remind you there is nothing wrong with technology. It can be a force for good, but the way it is presently being used, it is working against good and promoting thoughts, feelings, and behaviors that diminish our value as Christians, keeping us in the closet, relegating us as Saints of Vapor, with little substance, ineffectual, making us into ghosts without a voice.

Today almost every child has some sort of handheld device, but when we were children not only did our parents have rules about watching television but I also remember that at 11 o'clock at night or maybe midnight the stations would go off the air! That's it! No more television, it's over for the day. Now the stations run all night, with little interest for the saints, I hope; but a garbage can full of interesting programming to idle time, soothe and comfort anxiety, and excite imaginations and hopes.

When I was a child, we were busy creating memories as a family. The family mattered more then, I believe, and as Saints of Gold, we need to find a way to reconnect with our family and community.

I've noticed that the media is even replacing our attendance in church. People want to go to their television to watch sermons and evangelists, and we're allowing the television to take over our participation, our being in church together as a family and with other members of our church family, once again restricting our personal interaction and involvement with each other. The TV is giving us our ministry.

Certainly television can be a good medium for some people, for those who can't get to church because of the distance or because of their health, and it certainly is more comfortable to stay at home and listen to the words of the minister in our living rooms, but is this really the optimum way to receive the Word of God? Is this a truthful way of being part of Christ's community or is this a false way of feeling involved, of pretending that we went to church and participated as Jesus intended? How can the present-day church help us be authentic with our engagement of God's laws? How can the Saints of Gold invite authentic engagement with people who need God's full presence in their lives?

Then there is also the tremendous amount of devotion given to pop culture celebrities who use their fame to further weaken the fabric of our society and our nation. I'm talking about the Hollywood celebrities we see in the movies and on television, the star athletes in the NFL, NBA and other sports, and the musicians who promote drug use, sexual exhibition, antiestablishment views, self-aggrandizement, and resistance to all forms of cultural structure.

Again, my position on art and personal expression is one of tolerance, but not at the expense of the Kingdom of God. I believe in free speech, I believe in freedom of religion, I believe in social justice, I believe in the right of self-expression, but what I'm objecting to, and what I don't see, is equal time dedicated to the promotion of the gospel, of the need to heal ourselves and our communities through a devotion to God, the recognition in musicians' and artists' works about the importance of God in our lives, and celebrity behavior that promotes healthy relationships with God and with each other.

Why aren't more celebrities, whether Hollywood, sports, or musicians using their celebrity status to teach people a better way of living, a healthy way of building relationships and supporting communities, using their media power to model the expressions of spiritual health? Instead we feast on stories of multiple marriages and divorces, children born out of wedlock, fortunes earned and squandered, and the excessive and proudly showcased use of drugs and alcohol, etc.

Stop and think a moment and tell me who your heroes are. Not your heroes from the past like Martin Luther King, Jr., or perhaps the Kennedys, Ronald Reagan or Billy Graham, or other considered heroes like Tiger Woods, Oprah Winfrey, Taylor Swift, or how about Colin Kaepernick? Who are your heroes today? Who are the people with a national or international voice that you look up to? You'll be surprised because it'll take you a while to think of one. Can you name two? Three? It's difficult to do because in today's culture we don't have many, if any. No modern day heroes for the cause of the cross of Christ?

This is my concern. We are leaderless when it comes to knowing our path and following leaders who know where they're going, who know the Truth, and have the intention of leading us, encouraging us, providing us with the words and the passion to move in the right direction, to achieve our goals, to re-create the bonds that build healthy communities, restore families, and inspire us to generate self-worth.

As a Saint of Gold, what is your role in accomplishing these?

New Heaven and New Earth

It's time now for a new heaven and new earth. When you think about the old saints in the Bible, they didn't have a theory of evolution, or the Big Bang theory to think about. They accepted wholeheartedly that there was a Creator who created the heavens and the Earth, created the plants and animals, and created mankind.

Besides, it truly doesn't matter if scientists explain the scientific version of how the galaxies were formed and our solar system came to be. It truly doesn't matter whether or not we are biologically related to monkeys and prehistoric "ape men".

As I was thinking about it, once again God's Saints on Earth are being given the lie, and I believe we have unwittingly swallowed it, many of us, more than we should. What is the Truth and what is fiction?

The question that comes to my mind is how did the atoms and molecules that formed to become the stars, the planets, the animals, and humans get created? Something that's made has to have a Maker. Something cannot come from nothing.

Besides, as a believer, are these things we should even be tossing and turning in our minds? Do I really believe I need to take a position on how the Earth was formed? While it may be very interesting to ponder, the point is we know what the Bible says, and so we know that God created the Earth and everything on it. Instead of spending our time on puzzles that don't matter, we should be continually growing and gravitating to the Word of God so we can become better people in this world, become brighter lights and withdraw from the confusion of a debate with no meaningful purpose.

The Word of God is true, it's foundational, it's strong, and the Bible says for us to watch and wait. The Saints are being asked to look at what's going on with people and with the world and wait. Wait until the end? No, but wait until there is a judgment. As the world becomes more chaotic, people are going to need someone like us, like you, like me, the Saints of Gold, to help them understand what's going on around them and to guide them toward establishing or renewing their relationship with God and Christ.

Is the Bible True?

Is the Bible true, Saints of Gold? Is God truly offering His love? Does God offer love to the entire world of people and not just His children? Is there love? Is there a God? Is the Bible true? Is God real?

Lots of people want to know. The idea of God is too profound, and our minds can't comprehend the enormity of this Truth. We can entertain that there is a God because God has made us in His image and to be like Him in thought and mind. The concept is too big to understand, but I feel His presence and I'm thankful that I know Him from this. I feel His presence and that's the Spirit of the Lord which dwells inside each of us.

People get confused and say, "I don't feel Him, I don't hear Him."

I respond, "Well, you see His handiworks in the skies, in your mind and in the way that you think, in your understanding of the world. This is not something that came out of nowhere."

A father and mother shouldn't deny the presence of God. They should see God in their children as they raise them. Children don't just get born and then automatically start developing, having know-how and understanding and curiosity of life. Children are looking at you and mimicking you, as saints should be looking at God, and mimicking God. Children are evidence of God's presence, of God's hand at work. Unless adults are as little children, we miss it. Do you have child-like faith?

Is God real? Yes.

Is the Bible true? Yes.

Who says so?

God, He says so. God says, "I'm real."

Whether you believe it or not, that's up to you. It's an option you have. So, what do you think? You call yourself a Christian and a believer, so are you real? Are you true?

Our responsibility and our sacred duty as Saints of Gold is to keep trusting, and keep believing. In the days when the Bible was being created, men of renown, mostly men but there were a few women, too, who came together to put all these revelations and inspirations onto paper so the Words of Truth could illuminate our minds and hearts. God gave man revelations, He inspired them, inspired all these people to do what they did, and they put God's Word to paper, and they wrote about God and His Son, and then we receive the illumination as we read the Word of God into our hearts.

Because of the unhealthy society in which we live, because we have grown weak from the onslaught of the media and the erosion of our stamina due to the endless repetitive and typically harmful messages we see and hear dozens or hundreds of times every day, we tend to forget that God is the source of life and of every aspect of our lives.

Because we've grown weak and became isolated, we begin to surrender and stop trusting, we stop believing and allow doubts to materialize because we stopped reading and stopped spending quality time with the Word of God and with other Saints who can reinforce our beliefs with their own determined and honorable examples.

As people of God I think we don't read the Word of God enough to receive that illuminated feeling, the feeling of deeply knowing He is my Lord, He is my King, He is my All in All. We lose that personal relationship when we diminish or stop spending time with God, with His Word, with the Bible. As Saints of Gold, we are all theologians when we study God's Word. When we stop reading the Bible and we stop spending quality time with the Word, it's like not spending quality time with your children and not knowing your child the best way you could know him or her. When this happens, something important is lost, and your connection and participation in a critical relationship in your life is weakened and may even be destroyed.

We are blessed to have the option to know God, to believe the Bible is true and that God is real. As Saints of Gold, we are called to rise up knowing that God is powerful and that we have that power which He gave us through His Son.

I wanted to know the definition of God and so I found this from the *Westminster Catechism*. [1]

> "There is but one only living and true God who is infinite and being in perfection. A most pure spirit and visible without body, parts, or passions. Immutable and man's eternal incomprehensible almighty, most wise, most holy, most free, most absolute, working all things according to the counsel of His own immutable and most righteous will for His own glory. Most loving, gracious, merciful, long-suffering, abundant in goodness and truth, forgiving iniquity, transgression, and sin. The rewarder of them who diligently seek Him and with all most just and terrible in his judgments, hating all sin and who will by no mean clear the guilty."

This is who God is. We tried to comprehend, and He gave us a mind to understand and to want to know, to develop wisdom and knowledge. But when you are lacking a support system with your church and you are lacking a support system with other Saints, and your only resource is from the media, the Internet, television, and poorly behaving celebrities, then you're going to be less effective in a world that's dying.

Anyone in their 30s or older can look around and see the slippery slope and how much things have changed. They've changed immensely. The deterioration has sped up and we must keep our eyes and ears open because there is a very real enemy that's living among us. The devil and his minions are always at work, and our eyes and ears have to open up so we can protect ourselves, our children, nieces, nephews and all those we love and care about, and even better, the people all around us. This pervasive threat is viral and it influences people in our workplaces, our neighbors, the schools, the government bureaucracy and yes, our homes, too… We have to be vigilant to protect ourselves

---

[1] *Kelly, Douglas F. (1994). "The Westminster Shorter Catechism". In Carlson, John L.; Hall, David W. To Glorify and Enjoy God: A Commemoration of the 350th Anniversary of the Westminster Assembly. Edinburgh: Banner of Truth Trust. ISBN 0-85151-668-8*

from this disease while also shoring up our defenses and renewing our faith by reading the Word of God and congregating with other Saints so we can draw from their strength and contribute our own.

While times are different and dangerous, it is also a very exciting time and I want you to realize as you read this book that it is time for you as a believer to come out of the clouds, to come back down to reality, to confirm in your heart that God is Lord and He has chosen you to do His work! We are an army!

Saints and Aints

Who are the Saints? Raise your hands!

Who are the Aints? Please sit down.

If we were to take a poll, most people would probably raise their hand and say, "Yeah, I'm one of you guys." No one wants to admit they're an Aint.

Well, we can see that you're not an Aint, but you're a bad representation of a Saint. You're certainly no Saint of Gold, and not a Saint of Silver, and frankly, you're not even a Saint of Bronze. You're a counterfeit, and though you try to put on the costume of a Saint of Gold, you're really a Saint of Fool's Gold.

Fool's Gold looks real but when you wear it long enough, it tarnishes. It's not going to stand up to the test of time.

Aints are those who profess to follow the Word of God. God said the goats and the sheep will dwell together, but how do we know who's who? The way we can tell is because we talk with each other and because we have our eyes and ears open. By being observant and spending time together building relationships, we have the opportunity to assess each other's character and find out if a person is a Saint of Gold or a Saint of Fool's Gold.

God wants us to build relationships and as people cross our path we can ask questions. They may be offended, and they may not like what we're asking, but if you're in a burning building and I'm here to help pull you out, you're not going to say, "Don't save me!"

You're not going to tell me that because you want to die, you're just telling me that you're okay where you are, not realizing, not understanding, not knowing that you're going to die an eternal death. You're going to be apart from God, apart from the Savior

Aints rationalize and make excuses. When you listen to these people you can get a sense of where they really are in their walk, or if they're walking at all. They rationalize and ridicule and deny things in the Bible and truths about God. These are red flags that warn us we are interacting with a not-Saint. This kind of behavior lets us know that we need to pray about how to handle the needs of people who are not Saints. As Saints of Gold, we can't be afraid to speak up when we see hypocrisy. God doesn't give us the spirit of fear. We have to be stronger than we were in the closet. We have to speak out and say what we think and feel and believe. We don't have to be obnoxious about it, we don't have to be angry, we don't have to be rude. But we do need to speak with the voice God gave us to speak His Truth. We do need to earn our gold reputation. We do need to stand up for our beliefs so others can learn from us and become solid gold models themselves.

Remember, Saints of Gold can address issues, concerns, questions in a loving way. We can catch more flies with honey than vinegar, but we need to act with clarity, with confidence, with wisdom, with kindness, love and compassion. Before we speak, we need to find the voice of God that waits within us, we need to check the voice of our ego at the door. As a Saint of Gold, in our own imperfect way we are God's representative of his Word and Truth and Love. We need to allow the Spirit of the Lord to ignite and illuminate our heart because then we will speak from a higher standard, be more capable of saying the words God wants us to say and be more capable of saying the words God wants others to hear.

The Devil Is Real

Is he real? We have seen him in cartoons, we have characterized him as a mythical red devil with horns and a pitchfork, but no, he's not real. He's just a figment of our imagination, a mythological creature.

Yet, too many believers don't understand the power of who we call Satan. When our hearts and minds are so caught up with the ephemeral things of the world, it shows how much of a stronghold Satan has on the people of the Earth. The world has such a strong and hypnotic appeal, and we can't deny this. The physical world is beautiful, and it appeals to our senses in a variety of ways, seducing us with the pleasure it eagerly affords. We can't deny the effect the physical world has on people.

As Saints of Gold, we must be careful not to give authority to false salt and false light. For example, when people talk about meditating as an Eastern practice for communing with God, that is false salt. When people practice yoga as a means for connecting with God, that is also false salt. There's nothing wrong with meditating or yoga, but not as a way of establishing a true relationship with God.

The minds of natural men are easily and quickly diverted to false practices because the super-natural man is dormant, the minds of believers are dormant.

It's clear to me as it must be clear to you that the Adversary is prowling around. He has followers, people who have sold out and accepted non-belief as their path. One of the more recent and latest aired television programming is called 'Lucifer'. What do you think about that? Right here in Washington State, the national Wiccan conference was held. The good witches..... Good witches? That's demonic. That's not something that God and Jesus promoted! These practices do not fit in the gospel. You won't find references in the Bible of these kinds of practices being godly.

Saints of Gold realize that those who don't stand up for the Truth are surrendering their salt and light. The Adversary is real because there are people who are committed evildoers. There are also believers who are casual with their faith and have not yet committed to their sainthood. The Adversary has followers, and skeptics unwilling to commit to the Word and practices of God, and naïve people who lack experience and wisdom and have not found their way to the Truth. All of these people are in the devil's camp making fiction and non-truths.

This isn't the only army the Saints of Gold face because there are also enemies within that need to be recognized and expelled so our army of Saints can be effective and make an impactful difference in this world.

I talked to a lot of people and they have a hard time grasping the Truth because of all the interference from false messages and the pressures of living in our current culture. I am seeing Christians falling away from the Truth of God. They don't have a firmness of faith, they are waffling in their belief and aside from the emotional strain of whatever situation they may be in, this is why we need one another.

As you can see, the days are getting tougher, and the Bible says to encourage one another because it's so easy to get off-point with all the illusions and false leads that cross our path daily. Unless you have cultivated your relationship, like learning to speak a language or play an instrument, you're not going to get good at being a Saint. You're just not. Being a Saint of Gold is an intentional and willful practice, and if you don't have the will, you can say, "I don't have the will, Lord. Please help me to have the will!" That's the prayer. "Give it to me, Father." And if you don't want it, then say, "Lord, please take the "don't want"! Take it off of me!"

There are some strategic prayers, I think, and we have to know this stuff!

You can't be a baby when you're 50 years old and say you've loved the Lord for 25 years. Apparently something wasn't right and you missed out on some important information for nourishment and growth. Recognize that and examine yourself. Don't beat yourself up about it, but make it right now. Become fully committed with the Lord even if the last 25 years have been lightweight. Just because you went to church all this time and you say the right words, it doesn't add up. Let others see or feel your Sainthood. You were in the habit of pretending to be a Saint, but you have not been authentic and internalized your participation in God's community as a Saint of Gold.

You can be a Saint of Bronze, and you can become a Saint of Silver, and you can keep working on yourself and become a Saint of Gold, as pure as 24 carats if you wish. I hope you do. We need you to be that Saint, we need you to speak the Word of God, we need you to spread the good word and make disciples.

Those Aints that have gold flakes all over them, they will be seen as empty Saints, and those that are wandering around aimlessly and not keeping an alertness about them or responding in a positive way to the people God puts in their path to help them know and understand will also be seen as false salt and false light.

I'm excited to be in this time. Since God is sovereign and omnipotent and omniscient, which I believe, meaning present everywhere and knows and sees everything, then He has allowed us to be here at this time, to be a part of the world during this time. I'm very excited about that, and being able to talk about these kinds of things, to give people a heads-up and an alertness, and awareness and a change of attitude about what's going on around them. I don't think it's being talked up enough and that's why I've written this book, to inspire and ignite your spirit to let you see and know that there are people with strong faith taking meaningful action, but there are not enough of us, and I think if more of us talk about our faith and our need to be active and influential, there will be many more people evangelizing and bringing God's Word to those ears that are meant to hear the call.

It's such a privilege to write this book and evangelize the message I've been given. He is the one who changes hearts. Unless God draws you, you cannot come to Him, but it's great to know we can be a part of what God is doing on Earth.

So, is it true there is a God? Do you believe that, or is it false? And all of the facts and information that is being presented to us through the media and the great variety of sources, I would say just be careful. I advise that you filter it through what you know about the Word of God and make sure you are on point. And again, don't spend a lot of time on the screens, spend it in the Book. That's the Book of God, the Bible, spend your time there.

We are an army of believers called The Saints and we're moving and impacting and we're making a difference in the world! The devil may be real but he has nothing against the powers of the army of the Saints. Amen?

PRAYER:

> *Father in Heaven, You are Omniscient, Omnipotent and Omnipresent. Thank you for the truth from on high that sets the Saints apart from others. Forgive us when we forget to act upon and walk in Your Truth.*
>
> *We are no longer being tossed to and fro by lies, untruths and the trickery of men with false teachings, cunningness and craftiness. Forgive us for our ignorance and laziness of believing half truths when we have the whole truth through Your Word. I pray that we become better Saints as the ambassadors You have appointed us to be. Thank you, God, that Saints of Gold people are steadfast, immovable and always abounding in the work of God, knowing that our labor is not in vain.*
>
> *In Jesus' Name I pray.*

Chapter 6

Enemies Within

Battle of the Mind

The last chapter was about the difficulties Saints face from the influences of our culture and society, which is heavily materialistic and competitive. This chapter focuses on the battle against the mental and emotional distractions Saints need to overcome, influences we create in our own lives and the lives of others unknowingly or intentionally.

I am reminded of Ezekiel 11:5...

> "For *I know the things that come into your mind,* every one of them."

Of course God knows everything, knows all our thoughts and all our feelings. God is our sole source of light and energy and of everything we need so we can be His Saint and do His work on Earth.

When I think about the Saints of Gold and the gold they represent, I remember that the rocks need to be crushed and washed, and then the gold specks are gathered and eventually transformed into gold jewelry. It's the same thing with our lives, because God refines us and eventually we are transformed into devoted Saints who are educated in His Word and inspired to do His work with those souls we meet along our path.

I am thankful to have a healthy mind and I thank God for the many who do as well. My mind is healthy enough to understand that there is a battle of the mind, the negativity of our mind, will and emotions one can face, and the stresses and strains that can lead to mental challenges and sometimes an eventual breakdown into mental illness.

God already knows what we're going to go through in this life, and He also knows what we're capable of handling and according to Him, it all works itself out for our good if we are the children of God. When we're caught up in the noise of life, and difficult people and upsetting experiences occur, we don't always know why these negative experiences have happened or how we're going to work through them, but the underlying truth is that God knows, and God gave these experiences a purpose for us.

Ultimately these negative experiences are spiritually positive and are for our own good, even when we can't see it. God's thoughts and ways are incomprehensible. "How can terrible situations and difficult circumstances be good for us"? This is where our faith and our trust as Christians are tested, and Saints of Gold rise to meet the adversity with their inner strength and commitment to the Will of God.

Yes, there are times when we have to accept that we live in a crazy, upside-down world, and the enemy, which I will call the devil, is actively pursuing to be within our thoughts. If the devil can't read our minds…how does he get into our minds? What causes him to come into our minds? What causes us to allow him in if we have the mind of Christ? How do we open ourselves up to this when we have negative thoughts?

Negative

Based on my own experiences, it's normal to have negative thoughts and negative emotions; we are human. God's teachings show us and teach us how to have a positive outlook on life and toward each other in spite of the human argument that sometimes goes on inside us. God knows the harmful thoughts we have in our mind could prevail and stay there, but God wants us to use the spiritual ability and power He has given us to dismiss thoughts and emotions that are negative and of no use. God doesn't want us to be bogged down with the cares of this world and keep negativity in our minds and hearts. The negativity could stay there, and often does much longer than it should; but God certainly does not want that for us. God needs our support to move it out, to banish it. God says you must become like Me, not in a literal sense, of course, but as a Saint that works on herself or himself, who is consistently mindful of the Word of God and as much as possible, aware of the intentions of God as evidenced in our thoughts and actions.

As a Saint, you are set apart; you are gold in the eyes of God. When you think about gold, what does that mean to you? How do you see yourself expressing your Sainthood during your day? The enemy within is always handy and will say to you, "That doesn't make sense!" or "How can you think of yourself as a Saint when you know what you did or what you thought?" These are the battles of the mind, the spiritual warfare that tries to oppress us and keep us from achieving the full potential God has given us. God wants us to use the gifts of our potential to benefit ourselves and others, healing ourselves and being available with right mind and right heart to heal those around us.

Positive

We have to learn how to look at things in a positive light. We have to become strong enough and smart enough to recognize the devil within and shun him from having influence over us. One of my friends always tells me, "Annette, you're such a positive person. You're always cheerful and so affirming with everything. When I'm feeling unhappy or discouraged, you look at the things I'm saying and turn them around and make them positive. I'm not like that."

Yes, we are like that. I am no exception. We can all choose to turn our minds around…or not. We can all choose to be positive, or we can choose to be negative. It's as simple as that. We can turn everything around instantly if we choose. We can turn our thinking on and off just like that when we desire, so let's start now and make the change from darkness to light, from negative to positive, from isolation to community, from living in the closet to being a visible inspiration to those around us.

God says we can either be foolish about this and prideful, or we can live in that wonderful childlike innocence which we were born into, and say to ourselves and others, "Yes, I believe. Yes, I'm going to make this change. Yes, I'm going to think and behave like this. Yes, I'm going to be able to do the right thing at the right time. Yes, I'm going to reject the fear, doubt, and discouragement I've put on myself and which I've even let others put on me."

And God is saying, "Yes, I'm going to wait. I'm going to be patient for my child to come back to me."

This is the battle. This is where the enemy lies within. The battle our army of Saints faces is with the process of sanctification, purifying ourselves from the dross we have gathered and accepted during our walk through life. All of that garbage and nonsense is not native to who we are as Saints of Gold, but rather the mud and stains we have collected from the social and cultural playground we lived in before we recognized and committed to the Word of God. Now, however, when we surround ourselves with the right influences and the right messages, the company we keep will provide the right encouragement to continue our work in God's name for His glory.

The responsibility for living a wholesome life is our own, and we need to feed ourselves by reading the Bible, meeting with and talking with other Saints, enjoying a steady diet of the Word of God and behaving like gold with every step we take throughout every day and night, 24/7.

The time for self-sabotage is over. Though we tend to dwell more on the negative than the positive, we can train ourselves to increasingly see the light more than the dark. As you move more and more into your role as a Saint of Gold, pray for yourself and say, "Father, I pray you will give me peace." As I look around during my day and see people afflicted with struggles and their own self-induced troubles, I automatically pray for them with the same words, "Father, I pray you will give them peace."

Real Mental Issues

Another battle of the mind that Saints sometimes face is the very real mental issues in the people around us. When I see the homeless people in my city, some of them look like their minds are confused, distorted, and disoriented. These people are suffering from exposure to the elements and emotional crises in their lives, and I understand that many of them are suffering from addictions with alcohol and drugs. I often wonder what Saints think when they walk past people like this, people who are living with chaos daily and seeking or not seeking help and recovery.

I also know that sometimes Saints also suffer from mental afflictions, and suffer emotional highs and lows, a mixture of exhilaration and depression, and a variety of emotional states. Not too long ago I happened to run across a website from a psychiatric association and I spent some time reading their material, gathering information from several different websites. It seemed to me there was a lot of media hype about psychiatry, and I became aware that much of the practice of psychiatry is not structured in a way God would have mankind deal with mental disorders such as sadness, emptiness, hopelessness, loneliness, etc.

I can see that mental issues are quite real, and sometimes these might best be treated with medicines and the guiding hand of trained and certified doctors. I also know and understand the realness of the enemy lurking around us, telling us we are defeated in our suffering, that we are deserving victims of our pain. The Bible, however, says we can have joy and peace in the midst of the suffering and pain in our minds. We can also become transformed by renewing our minds through our belief in God, and when we take on the mind of Christ. When you read the Bible, you see that Jesus also went through emotional states, and

Jesus experienced these human afflictions and rose above them not by being immune to these wounds as He might have done as the Son of God, but by placing His faith and trust in His Father, in our Father.

Doctors and Medications

Of course, doctors and medicines are necessary in life, but it's troublesome to me that our schools now have a tremendous variety of practitioners such as psychologists, psychiatrists, and therapists, many who quickly adhere to medical drug solutions. There are very young children under psychiatric care, and this tells me that the enemy has achieved some major inroads. The Bible tells us the enemy is lurking around to see who he might devour. We know we live in a fallen world and even though things happen in this fallen world, God is still sovereign here…but do we believe that?

Do you believe you are a real diamond or do you feel more like zirconium? Are you a gold nugget or a nugget of fool's gold? Are you challenging yourself to get the gold medal or are you settling for the bronze? The bronze medal is okay, if that's what you can have with all your efforts, but let's try to exceed ourselves and meet the gold expectation!

We've also heard the expression "the Golden Years". What is that all about? You've spent the majority of your adult life working and God has blessed you to live a long time, to become an elder. Too many of our elders spend their golden years doing nothing except relaxing. They're on the golf course or tending a garden, taking care of grandchildren… These activities are fine, but how are you also expending and expanding your life to achieve more in God's name, not just for your own family, but for your larger family of mankind? Being retired is wonderful because now you have time to do more for God and achieve the gold standard as a Saint of Gold.

Voices Heard

Sometimes people hear voices in their head. These voices can come either from God and His angels, or the enemy. As a Christian and as a Saint, you can tell the difference between the two voices you hear. We have to go beyond the sabotage of the enemy within, get past the negative thoughts and messages of our minds and do something more, be something greater for God, for the cause and for the Kingdom's sake, and use the strategies that are available to us. Are there strategies? You bet there are!

Warfare Strategies

There are a lot of strategies available to us. One of them is being around the right kind of people, people who are positive and uplifting, people who live their lives as true Christians. Another strategy is increasing your awareness and being conscious of what you are digesting in your mind, being careful to avoid the constant barrage of negative media messages. Your increased awareness should also focus on the kind of food you're eating, so it can be healthy and serve the temple of your body, keeping it free of disease so you can avoid a death that comes too early. Are you reading your Bible? How much sleep are you getting, who is influencing you, what are you watching on television or in the movies, what kind of music are you listening to?

Sometimes we forget to be mindful because the work of the enemy is so pervasive and strategic that it's easy to become numb and fall in line with the hypnotic behavior the enemy wants us to have.

Some of us also find it difficult to think of ourselves as Saints, and don't like to wear that label. I grew up with the term "Saints", so it comes naturally for me. My father often talked to his congregation about our being the Saints of God. Because people sometimes feel inadequate, they feel they aren't worthy to be seen as a Saint, and while very few of us reach the status of Peter, Paul, or James, there's nothing wrong with also seeing ourselves as Saints because we need to understand who we truly are and what our purpose truly is. Note that Peter, Paul and James were flawed men, and Paul stated he was the chief of flawed men.

Demons are Real

Demons are real, as is God. To me, the two go hand in hand. If you don't believe that God is real you most likely aren't going to believe that demons are real. Satan worshippers believe in Satan and not God. How foolish. Believe it or not, on Earth there is good and evil. You can see the conflict in almost everything around us. Movies and TV dramas, books and politics, the behavior of people around us are all evidence of the struggle between good and evil.

Recognizing that evil exists is very important because not only does good show itself more clearly in the face of evil, but also we need to be prepared to support the good we see in people as well as help them force out the demons afflicting them in their lives when we can.

There are many types of demons. Some demons are more serious than others, of course. Excess of anything is a form of evil. Alcohol, drugs, compulsive sexuality, greed, non-truth, excess eating, excessive shopping…all these things comprise just a few of the addictions and ungodly activities people around us are doing. You and I have also engaged in some of these activities to our discredit, except we know better now, we can tell fact from fiction now, and we are doing our best daily to live in the truth of God's Word.

Just as we are trying to do the best we can, so also should we encourage those around us to do their best as well and continually do what we know God wants us to do with good and proper behavior in thought, feeling, and deed.

Meditation

I've always been curious about people meditating. What are they meditating on and what are you meditating on? The definition of meditating is to "think deeply for a time", so it's good to meditate on these things: whatever is pure, whatever is lovely, has good rapport, and has virtue. Meditate on these things!

Have you noticed how widespread Christian yoga has become today? This is an example of how closely the line between Christianity and physical or meditative practices has become. The dividing line is being blurred and the authenticity of God's Word may be compromised by this mixing. I'm not saying there's anything wrong with Christian yoga, but if it's truly Christian, why does it have to be yoga? Let's just call it what it is. It's Christian exercise, period. It doesn't have to be yoga.

The world has capitalized on so many things that come from our heavenly Father, and many of our so-called leaders take the easy road because it becomes more comfortable to just go along with the flow and do what everyone else is doing…and call it Christian! Just put the Christian tag on it! The problem is that when we do this, we're not really seeking wisdom and understanding, we're not really focusing on God's Word and His expectations for us. We're not really being authentic, or uniquely and wonderfully made individuals. We are distracting ourselves or fooling ourselves and each other that we are behaving in a Christian way instead of seeing that this is largely a hollow experience.

We have to remember there are two kinds of people in this world. There are God's people and those that are not God's people. We're supposed to be the difference between the Children of Israel and the Gentiles who didn't understand that God's people were being separated to keep them from being contaminated from the unclean behaviors of the world. Now, we as Saints are being contaminated more and more, almost to the point of being given over! The enemies within strengthen against us as our vigilance decreases.

God, in His purpose, has given us over to our undisciplined minds. God has given us the free will to move in this wrong direction, and it is by the grace of God that God is still with us in spite of our worshiping the idol of fool's gold.

Can this situation change without our seeking Him? No, it can't. It can't change unless we knock at the door of His heart. Can a change occur without our asking? No, it won't. God tells us to ask, seek, and knock. There can only be a change when we recognize the error of our ways and the Truth of His calling. Then there can be a change, and we can help each other to change. Are you willing to change? Are you willing to help others change? I'm crying out for help. Will you help me?

The Helmet of Salvation

The helmet of salvation is the process of our sanctification. We put on the helmet of salvation to help us in our battles with the enemies within.

When we ride motorcycles and bicycles we have to wear helmets in case we crash. It is a protection and our means for deliverance. The helmet of salvation also protects us by blocking out the noisy distractions of our Earthly life so we can hear the Spirit of the Lord speaking to us from inside the helmet. His voice is very soft and very sweet, and it helps to keep our minds whole, to help us remain positive and stay golden in our awareness, in our thoughts and actions.

Relaxing in the Word

With our helmets on, hearing the Word of God more clearly, we can relax in the Word. The Word keeps us strong and our minds steady, at ease and calm. God said He will give us peace in the midst of the storm, and His Presence provides the steadiness, the calmness, the dismissal of our fears and our relaxation in the comfort of His grace and love.

This is what the Word of God provides us, and yet people aren't seeking God's Word as much as they could, as they should, when they are afflicted with troubles. I think the problem is we're listening to too much television, seeing too many errant messages on the Internet, listening to the words of devils who say the Word of God is a lie, or craftily misconstruing the real truth of the Word. "Be faithful and committed and win God's approval in studying the Word, not being ashamed of the true message."[1] The Word is our sustenance. The Word is our source. How much intake of it do you get?

Faith and Grace

Faith and grace are two of the most important gifts we have as Christians. We believe that faith and grace are active in our lives and their combined influence provides super-natural transformation so we can have the kind of life that has been promised to us.

There is no doubt that this is not an easy life. Everyone you see will sooner or later have conflicts that cause damage and wounds. It's not an easy life because by our very nature we are sinners not sinning, and suffer from the afflictions of death, illness, wrong desire, pride, etc.

We are born to constant warfare, to constant battles and challenges. There are hundreds or thousands of influences that assail us in our lives, coming to us perhaps from our parents, our children, other family members and friends, our jobs, and of course, our internal negative thoughts. There are challenges, there are casualties, and there are times when will be severely injured.

When we're in the midst of a serious battle, we must remember that safety, harmony, peace, and joy are also available to us during the battle, on the battlefield. We can have relaxation in our minds even as we are conflicted, even as we see the challenges those around us are going through. We can have an ease about it when we choose to use our faith and call upon the grace of God. No matter how severe the battle is, the battle and its outcome can be different when we remember the Word and call upon God to relieve us of the enemies within and without, also remembering that the battle is not ours. God truly wants to be the Commander-in-Chief.

We don't have to accept grief, loss, pain, guilt, and suffering as hopeless life experiences. Our experience doesn't have to be filled with

---

[1] Paraphrase of 2 Timothy 2:15

the awfulness of these conditions. We can choose to make the battle a pleasant and even a positive experience because our faith and the grace of God is greater, more powerful than any corrupt condition facing us. Those who understand will know what I mean, and those that don't, won't. It's the difference between something that is genuine and something that's fake, and we all have that inner knowledge when we listen. We all know when something is real and something is fiction. When it's real you should know it and when it's fake, you should know that, too. Faith and grace are two of the most powerful instruments you can use to overcome life's constant assault.

Learning in the Church

Another vastly important tool is the learning you can receive from attending church. When you are around other believers who can help you learn and grow and you receive the safety, unity and harmony of being in a congregation of other people who believe as you do, you will experience personal and spiritual development and benefit from peace of mind. Yes, it is possible to have this experience outside the church, and you don't need to be a Christian, but by attending to your learning in the church, you will have a biblical understanding of your purpose.

There's something else at the end of your life that's waiting for you and it's bigger than we know. It's more than we know, and we can gain a little bit of understanding and truth about it if we're willing to lower our guards, open our ears and eyes, and learn. Jesus said to learn from Me, but He transferred that to us. We need to learn from one another in truth and in love, and learn together. Let's receive and live the fruit of the Spirit.

One of the fruit we need is the absence of long-suffering. This affliction will stay with you until you've made a transformation and say, "Get the heck out of my life! I'm done with you!" We have the power to do this for ourselves, and we can also pray for a person to be set free and made whole, starting in their mind. Becoming that Saint of Gold is really an inevitable process. Isn't it?

Not Conforming to the World

As Saints of Gold, we're not supposed to conform to this world. We don't want to. I know I don't want to conform to this world but more and more the world is saying, "Yes, conform to me. Come to me. I want you. You don't have to exercise. You don't have to eat healthy foods. You don't have to go to church. You don't have to reach the goals you set for yourself. You don't have to make any adjustments to the way you're living. Relax! Just be as you are. Get comfortable because it's rough out there, and you're okay."

That's what the world is saying to us and I feel this lulling hypnosis has led to where we are today. I didn't expect to see the world look like this in my lifetime. I really didn't, but God is moving forward with this rapid decay, moving forward so fast that many people won't be prepared when the time comes and God decides to "do something". Enough is enough!

When is that "something" going to occur? We don't know when, but we need to be steadfast and immovable, we need to be growing, we need to be challenging one another, we need to be unafraid to speak in love and truth to people about what they're doing and what they're not doing. We need to remind Saints that they are ambassadors for God in His world.

We need to be good models when we carry the Word of God, we need to get our bodies in shape, have our minds made whole, get connected and stay connected, keep our mind focused on our purpose and our responsibilities. We need to fix our minds and our intentions on something higher, something grander, something beautiful and not conform. When we avoid conforming to the popular culture and stretch ourselves, we can be transformed and perform the miraculous. Thy will be done on earth as it is in heaven.

Stresses and Strains

In the meantime, we have to be strong enough to handle the many stresses and strains we'll face. The culture we live in is very alluring and strong and we need to develop all the muscles and skills, our strength of spirit and our knowledge of the Word of God to overcome the resistance people have about making positive changes in their lives, about accepting God and Jesus in their lives, about forsaking the desires and behaviors encouraged by the media and by the world, and rely on the Truth to help us grow and stay strong and face the world's obstacles with our unbreakable faith and the grace of God.

Treadmill of Success

Have you ever asked yourself the question, "Is a hamster on a treadmill getting any pleasure from running round and round and staying in the same place?" He probably is because he's so used to doing that, just like the people you see around you who are locked-in on their little pleasures and comfortable lives.

We need to be like that hamster on the treadmill, except our treadmill needs to be our treadmill of success. There is value in continuously and repeatedly building our success as Saints of Gold. We need to increase our connection with each other both in and out of church; we need to have strong bodies and sound minds. We need to think positive thoughts and maintain positive emotions. We need to deepen our understanding of Scripture and improve our ability to talk about it with others. We need to learn how to be better ambassadors for God, how to speak the truth and inspire people to seek out God and follow the path that Jesus set.

We can practice good habits even when we're exercising, and instead of listening to a headset with something less edifying, we can listen to what the Spirit is saying without a headset about ourselves and others and pray and ask God to intervene. We could pray about things that are not so lovely, we could pray about things that have not gone right, things that cause people to blame God or feel isolated from Him. We can pray about things that help us to develop and cultivate our minds to constantly think good thoughts of ourselves and others.

We don't have to let our minds betray us with complaints and naysaying like, "I can't, I won't." We don't have to let anxiety take over our minds, we don't have to fall into the traps of predicting something is going to happen that never does, we don't have to work ourselves up because we don't really know what's going to happen.

We can put on the helmet of salvation and calm ourselves, put our faith in front of us and remember God's promises to us and know we are forgiven and blessed. Then, once we are strong and capable of taking care of ourselves, we can teach others to know how they can do that as well, and they can calm themselves and transform the negativity that tends to consume most people, most Christians, most Saints. It overtakes them because they have not practiced those behaviors that give them strength, that fortify their faith.

Our lives are all about faith, and family, and community. A life that's full of purpose, that's cultivated and developed, is a life that's based on faith in God, faith in the Bible, faith in our responsibility to behave as God's ambassadors on Earth. We recognize our calling by the family God puts us in, by the children he gives us or doesn't give us, by all our family members and other people, too. It's about our neighbors, and not just our next-door neighbors but about everyone God has deemed necessary to introduce into our lives, and seek out the calling and gifting of our lives while we are here on Earth.

I'm glad God has awakened in me the desire to know more. I'm glad I have alertness and awareness of what this life is about, and I look forward to the next life because I believe in the Word of God. I believe that the Bible is true. I believe that the enemy is real, that the enemy denied the power of God and wanted to do "his own thing".

People always want to know why, but we don't have to understand why. Everything God has done is done for good, for our good, and it's all positive. He is a positive God! We must remember that we live in a fallen world so we're going to see and do negative things, we are going to be confronted with negative circumstances, but God is not negative at all. The point is for us not to conform to the world but to learn how to conform to the Will of God. Our responsibility is not to the world, it is to follow the Word of God in every way we can, and to continue improving ourselves so we become God's great ambassadors on Earth, His Saints of Gold.

Refresh Always

We need to constantly refresh ourselves in God, in God's variety of manifestations, and in the people of God. This commitment, part of our treadmill of success, has to be intentional. We have to remind people that just because they come to Jesus, they're not going to necessarily get the big car, the big house, and all the other luxuries Earth provides.

Coming to Jesus is more than that. It's a life that's difficult yet easy. The obstacles in our path may be difficult, but our ability to handle the obstacles becomes easy when we listen to God's voice within us and accept the encouragement, embrace the Word, and make ourselves whole and complete.

When we think differently, we receive different results. As a man or woman thinks, so they are. If I think I can, I will be able. If I think I can't, I won't. If others around me are thinking I can and I'm thinking I can't, then I need support, I need someone to help me until I get to the point where I, too, am seeing myself with the eyes of someone who sees me and truly cares about me. "Yes, you can, and I'm going to help you!"

PRAYER:

Father in Heaven, You are The Most High. You know the things that come into our minds, every one of them. Help the Saints to truly know and believe this to enable us to think on the good things, the lovely things, the things of virtue and capture those thoughts which are not of You. We trust in You for our health comes from You and we are not afraid of what the world is doing around us. We are more than conquerors in You against the things of the world. Saints are the head, we are above, we are blessed and highly favored by You. We have the mind of Christ and know Your voice, not another. Our complete armor will be put on to fight the battles that lie ahead of us. We will resist the devil and he will flee, because we have weapons that are mighty in the pulling down of strongholds. Help us Holy Spirit to meditate day in and day out, to enable us to not let our guard down in our thoughts against the evil one, because he would like nothing more than to destroy us in spirit, soul and body. We are not conforming to this world, but are being transformed constantly in the renewing of our minds with Your love and blessing.

In Jesus' Name I pray.

Chapter 7

Don't Be Caught Without This

Being saints, being people of God, we shouldn't be caught without the personality and character of God. We shouldn't be caught without the godly personality which is the fruit of the Spirit…love, joy, peace, kindness, goodness, faithfulness, gentleness, self-control, patience. Just as vegetables serve the body, the fruit of the Spirit is also a necessary diet. It's a spiritual food essential for the spiritual man or woman to develop and cultivate.

Love

When the Bible speaks about the fruit of the Spirit, the first one is love. We know, as people of God, and maybe even the world knows, that God is Love. In the same way, the world maybe even the people of God, will question and ask, "How can He do this? How can He let people starve or be persecuted and tortured if He is a God of Love?" The truth is that we don't understand the depth of God being Love. God is Love, but when we think of the word "love" we understand it as "human love" which is the love for our children, parents, family, and friends.

God's love goes so much deeper and further than human love. It really is an incomprehensible love to the point of God giving up His Son for us. His Son came down from dwelling with God in the heavens. He took on the personality and the character of man and became a man. Who can do that? God gave His Son to come here, to our corrupted world, and to even die for us. In our earthly reality, who would say, "I'm going to give my son over to you, Annette, give him up for your life because I love you."

It isn't going to happen. You're not going to give me your son in place of my death, are you? Yet, the Bible says this is the kind of love we should have for one another. It's almost impossible but there's a super-natural love that we, as believers, need to cultivate, a love beyond our own natural ability to love.

The characteristics of love are genuine and divine concern for others. When we say "genuine" we mean "realistic" and "truthful". It is to have concern and care for others and then act upon it.

Present Action

Saints of Gold should work to draw people back to their faith with love because without love we can't help one another. Without love, we can't improve our own lives or have any meaningful impact on others.

The Bible speaks of equipping us, the people of God, with great personality, talents, skills, and abilities that will make us an ideal workforce or team to do God's work. I question if we have the genuine care for people that's needed, especially in the workplace where we have a performance-based system that undercuts this level of cooperation, and instead encourages an attitude of "Well, I can't allow this person to outperform me because his performance is better and I might lose my job!"

I have tried to demonstrate heart-felt cooperation and it was truly hard, especially being supportive for a person who wanted to outshine me in every way. But God prepared me, in one way or another, to be ready for this situation. Prior experiences I'd had were like a training ground for me. I didn't know it then but when I reflect on it now, I sensed and understood the power of His love. As I sat in that office every day for five years, my awareness of that kind of love that God was teaching me grew exponentially.

I saw that God is our avenger. Because of His divine love for me and because I seek His guidance, comfort and peace, He enabled me, and even my colleagues, to have genuine concern for one another, which resulted in our establishing a healthy and reciprocal working relationship. I knew this when we reached a point one day when my once adversarial coworker defended me from being fired. He didn't understand it, but love conquers all, and God's love in me had conquered him. "I don't know what happened here, I really don't like her, but no, we don't need to let her go."

It's interesting how this spiritual kind of love connection developed and made itself present in the action of a person I knew didn't like me. He didn't want me to succeed and he didn't even want our boss to be concerned about or show care toward me, but God's love presented itself through his support for me at work, to his own surprise.

Love is goodness. Love is action. Love is showing goodness even to those who appear unlovable. We're going to have people, even in our family, who will be envious and jealous of us. Family members are not exempt. Having no preconceived notions, meeting our responsibilities and doing what we need to do, working together to build a better life, making things better for everyone, improving the system, working toward making society more supportive and more caring, improving the neighborhood by truly being neighborly…these are the actions of love and compassion, this is how Saints of Gold spend their time and personal energy.

The ultimate action for us as believers is to love God with all of our heart, mind, and soul. As a community of believers we need to talk about these things and how to mirror our personal and human image in the image of Christ. We need to see how short many of us fall in these areas, and I include myself in this accounting. The whole focus is to love God and then love our neighbors. For us to be able to do this we have to go back to the beginning, believing there is a God and coming to know Him… because how can we love Him if we truly don't know Him? We may have many acquaintances in our lives, but we may never truly know them. Get truly acquainted with God.

If we don't have that full heart, soul, mind, care, and concern about this Almighty Being who has a name and wants us to cultivate our knowing that He is a loving and caring God, then we can't cultivate the same level of loving for others and the necessary commitment of love won't work.

The message I'm focusing on is making sure that you, Saints of God and Saints of Gold, are truly sold on the fact that the Bible is true, there is a God, and there is an enemy that is against God. This enemy works against us to try to make us work against God, and if we don't have the unfailing purpose of loving God in our hearts with all our might, then all of what I'm saying in this book is senseless. Before you continue reading about joy and peace, please make sure you have a solid grasp of our purpose as Saints of Gold, and if not, then you must reread the first several chapters of this book!

Joy

With your heart aligned, now you can start experiencing joy. It's the highest joy possible, understanding who you are and that God has allowed you to be a part of His family. What does this mean?

Remember to make that commitment to yourself first, to love yourself. The primary principle of life is to love, even those who hate you or are against you. You must also love the enemy that's within you, too, that part of yourself that needs development, that needs refinement from base metals into gold. You must love all of yourself, so that every part of yourself can be included in your refinement toward becoming the most wholesome servant of God you can become.

What is joy? How can we even experience it in the midst of such terrible events happening in the world? How can people have joy when they are dealing with the earthquakes, tsunamis, hurricanes, wildfires and all the disasters that have happened in our nation and around the world? How can people grab hold of joy in the midst of chaos, confusion, and anger?

I believe it's a state of mind, and once we understand in our minds who we are in God, joy becomes internally and eternally available to us. Joy doesn't come from worldly circumstances but from knowing who you are in God. It's surrendering, obeying, and understanding that God is real and present in your life. When you have accepted Him in your life as your Sovereign God, that's when real joy takes place. For some people this is hard to do, but He said, "The joy of the Lord is our strength. The joy of the Lord is our help. The joy of the Lord is our peace." Nehemiah 8:10.

Going back to the analogy I've been using of processing gold from rocks through heat, I don't think we have yet gone through enough heat. If the nation as a whole would go through something terrible today, in the 21st century, I think we would quickly have a different and more thorough understanding of our lives and our purpose on Earth.

I believe there are a lot of people who experienced the hurricanes in the south and who, in one way or another, had a transformation in their hearts and minds and came to realize more profoundly their relationship with God. I think there are also some who have pulled further away from the truth of who they are because of their mindset or perhaps from the influences of the negative people around them. They are those who ask the how and the why. "Why is God, if He is loving, doing this to us? If He is loving, why did this happen to us?" They didn't go to the trouble of being reminded of His words, or the Christians and Saints are unable to help them remember the love that God has for us in spite of the fallen world in which we live, with all its difficult experiences and lessons.

The joy we are seeking is therapeutic.

> "A merry heart does good, like medicine,
> But a broken spirit dries the bones."
> Proverbs 17:22

I remember what I told my sister when she was crying and feeling sorry for herself. "You have the will to change the way you're thinking, the state of mind you have right now. You must remember and remind yourself who you belong to, that God loves you and He is in the midst of this with you now, in the midst of your sorrow and suffering,»

This is a practiced behavior. This is a practiced characteristic we need to cultivate and talk about to help one another. If we believe, as we believe in heaven and hell, that there's going to come a time when things will really get bad, when we might experience the worst of the worst here on Earth, if we are not conditioned or haven't cultivated the love and the joy of our souls, our mind, our spirit, many of us will fall away from the truth of who we are in God and in His love for us, and the love that cost His Son.

Commandment

The commandment is to be quiet and praise God. Think about people other than yourself; think about the nations that have no running water, let alone clean water to drink, and no food; think about the nations that have no reason to have love in their hearts, but do. Do we really think about those people on the other continents of the world? Or are we just focused on ourselves and our nation?

We, as Saints here in the United States, are losing ground. Not all of us, perhaps, but many of us are losing ground because many of us are not telling others that we're losing ground. Where is your joy? Where is your love? Where is your peace? Are you following the commandment to praise God, no matter what your circumstances?

Peace of God

"What is peace? How can I have peace?" a friend asked me. She was complaining about her troubles.

The peace of God is super-natural, and we must develop a super-natural mindset. Today's scientific culture puts a lot of emphasis on understanding the world around us, and yet we are still unable to understand the trillions of stars in the sky. Even the most brilliant of scientific minds falls short, and can't really explain the existence of stars, or the size of the universe, or how matter came to be. Who can understand God? No one! Who can understand peace? You can, if you truly know Him.

When my husband died, of course it hurt me terribly, but I did have peace. When my mom, dad, and my brother died, I was hurt and felt the pain of my loss, but there was a genuine peace that also came and comforted me, enabling me to sustain myself and go through the experience and arrive on the other side feeling calm and accepting. When death happens, people have to prepare for the services and deal with the many other "real" things before, once and for all, they can pick up their lives and move forward. How are you able to do this? You do it through your own will and through the super-natural power of God.

We are not alone, and you are not going through these experiences by yourself. Your will is being enabled by a super-natural power. I hear people say, "I don't know how people could have joy and peace without God." You may have joy and peace, yes, even if you are without God, but that joy and peace is something else, a different level of joy, contingent upon external situations and circumstances, and a peace resulting from the same externals. It's not at all like the utmost internal joy and peace you can have with God.

When you die, you will not have that hope of being with our loving Father for eternity. That's the difference. Yes, people can have joy, peace, and show love in action, like the philanthropists, for example, who give money and help the poor, but it's not like having Christ in your life. There's no hope of life after death, and that's the difference.

Sometimes they have more joy and peace than the Saints of Gold. I know a person in my neighborhood who is very contented, but not with the contentment of God; it's the contentment of self, which is very different. Her contentment is not focused on the inward man, that God-spirit that lives and dwells within us.

Going back to the fruit of the Spirit, we, the Saints of Gold, are fruit examiners for one another, but sometimes because our fruit isn't always so good, or as good as we wish it to be, we don't want to look at the fruit of another. We don't want to be compared and find our fruit is unripe or rotten, or falling off the tree with worms. Sometimes we tell ourselves, "I'm not going to say anything to you about anything because I'm feeling guilty about myself." Where does the shame come from? It doesn't come from God.

Will there be peace? Yes, there will be some semblance of peace but not what God has in store for us. The peace that He wants for His people, the Saints of Gold, is the peace brought about by that gold transformation, that powerful transformation of turning our hearts from rock to gold and being able to look inward and know who we are. It's that state of mind despite confusion, chaos, and anger. It's an action and a commitment that happens in the moment from being in touch with the God that dwells inside us.

Necessary

Is it necessary? It's the only way. It's as necessary as keeping our body healthy. It's necessary for us to have the love that we need, first for God, then for others. It's necessary to put that love into action. The goodness of the love comes when we're demonstrating our love. It's necessary to have joy, especially when you're in the workplace and you're burned out but still engaging with people while keeping the enemy at bay. Having that joy will keep you from getting frustrated, angry, and resentful about doing good, about doing the work of God right there at your job.

When we see other people not doing what they should be doing while we are working hard, without joy, we begin to compare and put on that weight. We become frustrated and then we regress to negative qualities, characteristics, or personalities. It's necessary to keep our minds focused on who we are, Saints of Gold. It's necessary to keep our hearts and minds praising and thanking God. It's necessary to be around like-minded people who encourage us. It's necessary to go to church so we can understand the love, to work on love with others, our brothers and sisters in the body of Christ so we can work on it more in and outside the family dynamics, and with the other people God put in our lives. It is necessary. These are necessary steps to help us improve as Saints of Gold.

Self Control

Don't be caught, first of all, not knowing who you are; that there is a God; that the Bible is real. Don't be caught without the love. He loved us first and that's why we love Him. A saint should never have the word "unlovable" in their mind or heart. A saint should not be heard saying, "I can't love them. I can't be with them. I can't associate with them. They're different than me." Instead, we should be embracing one another despite our different qualities and attributes. We have to help one another learn about the love of God. We should have that self-control and patience that enables us to have that endurance, that persistence.

One of the major problems with seeking joy is that we seek it from the wrong source. We don't understand that joy really comes from knowing and being a part of who God is and who He says we are for Him.

Are you feeding yourself with the gifts of God? Are you giving yourself the proper nourishment that feeds your soul? How do you give yourself the gift of being a true and free Christian? What are you doing every day and every moment of every day that helps you become the best Saint of Gold you can be? How are you providing the sustenance you need to walk through the joys and trials of life? How are you providing yourself with the strength and the love and the comfort you need in your life to be a source of kindness and compassion to others? How are you serving yourself so you can serve God?

There is the story of the lady who was married for more than forty years, and then her husband died. For several months, she sat alone in her home, sad and unconsoled. The shades were drawn, the doors were locked.

One day, after months of misery, she finally decided to do something about her loneliness and went to a pet store. She looked at the animals: cats, dogs, reptiles, and fish. She just wanted something she thought would be good for her and her loneliness. The owner of the store decided to show her a prized parrot.

She asked, "Does it talk?"

"Yes, absolutely. He's a real chatterbox and has a friendly disposition with a wide vocabulary. That's why this parrot costs so much, because of its unique qualities."

The lady bought the parrot and a cage. She brought the parrot home with anticipation for the companionship she was going to have, and it was going to be perfect because the parrot would talk with her and there would be an end to her loneliness and sadness.

But no matter how hard she coaxed the parrot, the parrot didn't say a word. The woman went back to the pet store and complained and said, "The parrot's not talking about anything. I'm not able to get a sound out of the bird."

"Well," the pet shop owner said, "maybe you should buy a mirror." The woman bought a mirror for the parrot thinking this would be the answer. Again, the parrot would not speak. The woman returned to the pet shop again, complaining.

"Well," the pet shop owner said, "maybe you should buy a swing." So she did, but still the parrot would not say a word. The woman returned to the pet store three more times, purchasing a bell, a little comfort blanket, and finally a climbing rope, all to no avail. To her horror and dismay, she woke one day to find the bird very weak and ready to perish without notice.

The woman returned to the pet shop yelling and complaining with the dead bird lying at the bottom of the cage and said she wanted her money back. She had tried everything, she said, and the bird had not even given one sound.

The pet shop owner said, "So the parrot never said anything?"

The woman thought a moment and then said, "As the parrot lay dying, I heard him say very faintly with his last dying breath, "Didn't they have any food at that pet store?"

PRAYER:

> *Father in Heaven, Your sovereign plan is for Saints to inherit Your Kingdom here on earth as it is in heaven. Give us this day our daily bread and forgive us our debts as we forgive our debtors, lead us not into temptation but deliver us from evil. Let the words of our mouth and the meditation of our hearts be acceptable to You because You are our Strength and our Redeemer. Help us to show love and give love in all that we do and say. We are a city on a hill with the brightness of light shining forth which cannot be hidden. We do not love as the world loves, but as You loved us by giving Your only begotten son Jesus. I thank you that true Saints are not routinely caught without living in love, peace and joy in You. I pray that we will rise to become Saints of Gold people who are limited to the trappings of darkness and walk in the light of Christ each and every day. Help us as Saints to exemplify a life of righteousness, holiness, and truth that is pleasing unto You, our Master and Savior.*
>
> *In Jesus' Name I Pray.*

Chapter 8

I Know Better But No One Saw Me

When I thought about how this book came to be, the topics, the headings, and the outline, a question popped into my mind. "Where did all these come from?" I even wanted to change them at times but I left them as is. I asked, "How did this all came about, Lord?" I felt like the Spirit of the Lord said, "I helped you with the outline and with the words that have filled these pages. This is what came forth, so now let it be as it is, Annette. That's how it's going to work and how we're going to present My message when it's all said and done."

Saints and Aints

Once upon a time we were all non-believers, the Aints, until we came into this awareness and knowledge about Christ and who we are in Christ. By accepting Him we were able to have the understanding of a Saint. Like a babe we grow up with that understanding. Then, we continue working on it in our lives as adults. We keep improving through others' influences, through circumstances, and through the teaching moments of situations.

I'll use myself as an example. I have done a lot of things based on the understanding that I grew up with as a child. People will often ask, "Why did you do that?" Well, the way we do things is because of our nature. Sometimes we forget that our nature is not golden and not solid. We have a corrupted nature and when people think they can control their nature all the time, they're misinforming themselves. By the grace of God, when we keep our minds constantly fixed on Him, and when we share some of the insights or expose the temptations we're having because we're in our natural state, we can ward off evil thoughts and maybe keep ourselves from doing what we would otherwise naturally do to our detriment.

Temptations

Temptations are normal to humans. All of us have them but the question is will we act upon them? We can try living with godly restraints, which is our self-control. This godly restraint doesn't come from us and may not work for us on our own. People can do the unimaginable, and we are capable of unthinkable evil. Think about the situations we've seen in the news the last few years, like mass shootings. I don't think these acts of extreme violence are driven by medication or mental illness. When you think about an average person who lies, steals, and gets angry, you think about someone normal, like you and I. People who behave in such horrible and truly evil ways may also have feelings of being unworthy or condemned by the people who once cared for them, and their emotions go out of control. They have succumbed to the devil within, and through their feelings of isolation and desperation they become a victim of the enemy in their heart and mind which then makes others a victim of these evil actions.

Thinking about the Ten Commandments, I can say that I have no excuse because I know better. I grew up with these moral lessons. I know not to steal and not to lie, but I've done that. I have stolen, I have lied, and the list expands when people are truly honest with themselves.

When you think about murder, it's not only physical murder but can also be a verbal one such as when your words carry gossip that murders and defames the reputation of another person. Think about the commandment "Honor thy parents". I believe that when we Saints were children we knew better because our parents taught us, but when we grow up, for whatever reasons, we begin to dishonor ourselves by ignoring God's commandments. We begin to forget that our days can be good upon this land when we obey this commandment. As an adult who should know better, we begin doing things that dishonor our parents' teachings, and of course we soil ourselves. Maybe our parents have no knowledge about the things we did but Someone is watching us. Someone is always watching us, and this we also forget.

Who is that Someone? That Someone is God. He is taking account of everything we're doing, saying, thinking and feeling. We forget that He knows everything. He knows the very thoughts we think, and the temptations we sometimes have in our minds, God already knows. He already sees them before we act upon them. He sent God himself, Jesus His Son, who came in the flesh to know our temptations as people.

People will try to question that if Jesus is God, how can He not be tempted? We have a tendency to focus on useless things, things that have no meaningful relevance to becoming a better person. For me it's like trying to understand math. I get a little lost in the calculations and the algorithms when all I really want to know, and need to know, is $4 + 4$ is 8. I just want to know how much change I'll get back if I give the clerk a \$100 bill and my cost is \$85. I just want to know how to add and subtract, multiply and divide. I don't want go further than that. I don't need to know or get lost in the calculus.

The essence and point of this book is to encourage us to go back to the basics. If we can't get the basics right, how can we then further establish our walk and be the people God called us to be? How can we go beyond the expectations people have in us as Saints? How can we do any of God's service on Earth if we don't have a true understanding of the basic foundation of being a Christian, and behaving like a Christian every day all day long?

These temptations, and this irritable dissatisfaction with life, this commercially-driven and hotly desired lusting in what the world perceives life to be is something we should clearly see is an illusion, as a false path offered by the enemy within, as a distraction from our purpose as Christians and Saints of Gold who know better, who must train ourselves and each other to know better how to respond to the temptations of our human and temporary life.

But since these desires are usually private and no one sees our dark and eager feelings and thoughts, we go on with them like everything is okay. No one knows because no one saw us thinking and feeling like people who had no idea about the Word of God and the omnipresent knowingness of our Father. As saints, we know better but we don't practice what we know. We allow these shadows to run underneath our physical appearance, and since this is so, do we really know better? By lying to ourselves, our sainthood is tarnished and the gold in our heart and soul diminishes.

Prayer is communing with God, intimately speaking with Him. It's spending quality time with God while looking within yourself, examining yourself, and making sure you are pure as gold. We should do this on a daily basis, several times a day. Communing with God in prayer, especially in times of temptation, is what we're supposed to do instead of thinking, "Well, no one will see me."

Think about your integrity. Take what happened to Wells Fargo as an example. This involved prestigious, powerful, and educated men and women who were working in a financial institution and who thought no one was watching them when they did whatever they did. Then, we see what happened in the news and the young people look up to see these older people living with untruths, ungodliness, and dissatisfaction with life. This is not the kind of message we want to give our young people, or each other.

Influences

Our influences can be our friends, acquaintances, or the social media. You may have heard of a fictitious character called Slenderman, which today's secular culture developed and presented to us. This dark and evil creature has become popular with some of our country's youth. As Saints, you know better than to allow your child to search Slenderman out on the Internet, or allow your children to go see a Harry Potter movie when it contains material that could mislead our children's thoughts and expectations. Ah, but no one's watching, we think, so we don't speak up about these influences and by keeping our silence we negatively influence either our children or our community, or ourselves.

Another monstrosity is this new show on television called "Lucifer". Have you heard of it? I wonder how long it's going to be on TV. We already have the Good Witch in its fourth or fifth season. Who watches this stuff? As Saints, we know better but when we sit alone on our couch at home and we think no one's watching, we watch these types of shows anyway. We don't watch them for any academic reason, so I guess people are watching them for entertainment because they are tired and unfocused, or they are allowing the enemy within to step forward and further distract us from our responsibilities as Saints.

Wouldn't it be better to read a good book, open our Bible and read about God and God's Word on Earth? Wouldn't it be better to listen to some uplifting music, or write poetry about the loving feelings you have for the people in your life? Wouldn't it be a whole lot better to take a long walk and meditate and ponder His goodness and say prayers about others? Wouldn't it be better to begin those music lessons and paint or take pictures like you have wanted to do? Go to hospitals or nursing homes and visit with others, go to the daycares, schools and see the smiles on children's faces, feel the love in your heart? Yes, I think this is all feasible!

Do you really have a committed and unclouded understanding of the Truth? Or are you letting your understanding of your purpose on Earth, of your purpose as a Christian, as a Saint of Gold get watered down by today's culture?

Maybe we are surrendering to the pressure of our friends and acquaintances who say we are acting "too Christian," or maybe we feel a sting when they call us "Jesus freaks", or this and that. I don't know. What do you think? How are you letting the social influences affect your behavior? Are you standing up or sitting down when it comes to your responsibilities as a Saint of Gold?

Am I Saving Face?

Maybe your life isn't representing the godliness of Christ and you have slipped so many times you're embarrassed or ashamed. Maybe you're putting condemnation upon yourself and your Christian friends. Even if this is the case, God is pleased that you're confessing, but does not want you to be in condemnation. Of course, be careful who you're confessing to because you might get ridiculed and shamed. Remember also, God will find the right person for you to confess to, but even if He puts you on a public stage and strips you bare, then so be it.

You may ask, "Am I going to be able to handle that kind of stripping?" Well, Jesus did. "Am I supposed to be like Him?" That's what the Bible says. "But no one's watching me anyway, so I really don't have to do all these things. I am a Saint, even though I'm lacking. I am a Saint but I can't do what you do. I can't be optimistic like you."

How come you can't? Why? When you let go of your ego and you acknowledge God in your life and Christ within, and you act on your knowledge about being a true and free Christian, you can do anything, you can be called to do anything God needs you to do. Saving face is neither here nor there because you are an instrument of God's Will. As a Saint of Gold, the only face you have is as God's representative, as a messenger for Christ.

Emotions of Feelings

Some feelings are negative emotions such as anger, shame, guilt, sadness, and unworthiness. I wrote about some of these briefly already. Sometimes life can be difficult and we look for succor. "With whom can I share my painful thoughts and distressing feelings to get a little bit of encouragement and help me get out of this unpleasant and harmful state I'm in? I want to reveal myself to someone. I want to reveal my loneliness, my lowliness, my dissatisfaction. I want to get some of these things off of me. Who do I go to?"

Go to God. Seek Him first but only if you believe in Him and diligently put His principles into action will you really do this. It is an individual intentional effort and your responsibility to constantly remember your belief; to internalize hope and build yourself up. We have to learn how to rescue ourselves, which we do first by staying close to God. We must surrender ourselves entirely to God. That's the rescue, that's the only real salvation.

Passive and Afraid

We can be, as believers, passive and afraid. The world is looking at us as a nation which is supposed to be leading in spiritual morality and behavior, but instead we watch quietly as our nation goes down the slippery slope to hell. God bless America. A well known pastor put it this way, "God damned America." The statement seems to be using the Lord's name in vain, as it were. But what was he really referencing when this statement or comment was made? What did he really mean by this? Yes, God established our nation and I believe this is historically so. Look at how this all came about. God has His hand on this nation. God has sent people from this nation to do His work, but here we are now, passive and afraid. What and who are we afraid of? We should know better. Stop this insanity. Salvation doesn't come through us unless God draws man first. It's not His Will that anyone should perish, but all should come under His saving grace.

How much time am I spending in the Word of God, the Truth of God, and in the power of God? How much time am I spending on social media, on my cell phone, on gossiping? We have busy lives, but they are not so busy that we cannot find the time to give God five minutes of our day. We may give Him an hour and a half on Sundays. That's ridiculous! Of the 1,440 minutes in a 24-hour day, you can't find 0.003% of your time, just five minutes, to spend with your God and Savior?

Time spent with God and with Christ is when we refuel ourselves. Find the time, okay? Go to church services on Sunday, go to a Bible study. You can't be a solo act or a twosome any longer. Offer your services to other Christians and to the non-Christians in your community. This is a much better way to spend your time than soaking ourselves up with prayerlessness, media hype, and all the secular distractions available on television 24 hours a day.

False Expectations

I think we forget who we are, and expect so much out of this life instead of setting our expectations on the next life. We expect that this life is going to provide us happiness, joy, and peace, and yes, this life can, and we can thank the Lord for that, but have the Saints lost the expectation of the next life? Do you truly believe there is a next life? If so, are you doing things today that will help you prepare for that next life?

It's easy to believe in the illusion and think, "I know better, but no one saw me. I know my mind should be fixed on God but hey, no one's watching me and no one knows me so I'm okay with refueling myself in God's presence for only a few minutes a week." If so, you're being lulled by the enemy within and by the culture around you, and you are not remembering that God is watching you. He sees you. He knows everything about you and what you're doing, and what you're thinking and feeling.

Belief in your own self-sufficiency is pride. When you're becoming overly ambitious for the things of this world, you might be overlooking that your daughter is already dating. Let's say she's fifteen years old and she's dating a 21 or 22-year old man, and you don't know. Did you overlook that because you were too busy going after false expectations?

We're being aggressive and trying to get…what exactly? A nice car, home, prestigious title, money? Are we trying to get all these worldly rewards thinking these will give us happiness, joy, and peace? Is that your expectation? Can you see how false that is? There's nothing wrong with being aggressive, with having a dream, a passion, a desire to have something more or do something more, or be something more in this world. But for whom are you doing this?

We often do it for ourselves, first; for others, second; for God, last. Am I doing these things with love in my heart or with hostility? Am I always angry because I'm trying to get ahead in this world? Am I putting others under the bus without a care about who I step on or step over to get there? Are we becoming like the world so much that we can no longer see, know, and understand we are first and foremost Saints of Gold?

We're supposed to be golden. We're supposed to be trying to accomplish this gold transformation process, going through the heat and coming out shining and polished. We're supposed to be the light on the hill. We're supposed to be the salt. Jesus says, "I'm good. Taste me. See me," and we, as Saints, should have that quality as well.

Greed and Dissatisfaction

There's nothing wrong with being concerned about how you look;

what you're doing; the kind of car you drive or house you live in; or how much money you're making BUT if all these things are just for you, that is greed. Do we covet what our neighbors have: a BMW or a Jaguar and a 3,500 square-foot house? When believers say, "People are looking up at me so now I want more than what they have," then they are lost to the world and have forsaken their true treasure.

Dissatisfaction is also a concern. I have been dissatisfied. Sometimes I catch myself being dissatisfied with this and that, when I do self-talk with, I believe, the enemy speaking in my head. Do you hear voices? Those mental voices? Are they the voice of God? Are they the voice of Satan? There's a blurry line there and sometimes it's hard to know.

Self-talk

I went to a psychiatric hospital once. I had never been in one before. This particular hospital was for teenagers, and I have to admit I was overtaken by fear. I felt the demonic oppression immediately upon my entrance inside the facility. I began to think in my mind, "Lord, this isn't of You. These people have mental illnesses, yes, they do, but Satan is running rampant in here and the people who are caring for them don't understand the extent of the evil that's here."

I was thinking about the spiritual aspect of this terrible environment when I suddenly noticed this young male patient looking at me, I felt scared and I started to feel uncomfortable. Then, I very quickly began to pray silently. I prayed over that young man, and whatever it was that I said in prayer, I sensed that something lifted off of him. I saw his countenance change and suddenly there was peace in his face. It was a weird experience, but I saw that self-talk matters and the authority we have in Christ proved very real once again and given for our use. How often is your self-talk laden with fear, doubt, and disbelief?

We must always remember to stay connected to our Divine source and sustenance, our hope, our deliverance, our safety net. Hold on to your safety net so you have more control over your self-talk. We have not been given a spirit of fear, but of power and love and sound mind to defeat the enemy within and out.

"I know better but I'm doing it anyway. I feel like no one's watching and this is really going to help me in the long run if I'm going to do (whatever ungodly thing you're thinking about) …" Not really, Saint. You are called from a higher authority, a higher power, and you are blessed to have that authority and power within you.

Remember, Someone is watching and that Someone is actually living inside of you. That's the Holy Spirit. If you, Saints, don't believe that, and don't believe there's a God, don't believe that the Bible is true, you're going to have trouble and become part of the trouble in this world.

I've listened to a lot of ministers and I like the ones who challenge me to go for higher holiness than the ones who water down the challenges. I prefer to listen to the ministers who challenge my heart to be more like Christ, to respond to a higher calling; to be a Saint of Gold; to get back on track with the things of God first of all in my heart, then, in my mind, and finally, in my actions.

Backbiting

Backbiting is speaking evil toward another, a slanderous and malicious talk designed to damage someone's reputation or even destroy them. We can do it quite well because we think no one is watching us as we do it. When we watch the news, we hear what people, even believers, are saying about the President of the United States. Don't be mad at me if I tell you that I voted for the man. Why? I will give you the reason: because I felt Gods guidance to choose Him over her. That should, then, just shut down the nonsense. They may ask, "So God speaks to you?" I would say, "Doesn't He speak to you?" I realize some things don't make sense to me or you, if we are being led by His Spirit. That was the case in my choice.

We gossip about a brother or sister with whom we haven't really shared anything, and we talk about indifferences we feel they have in their lives. That's displeasing, and that's not good. Remember, God is watching. He knows that you know better, but you are not interested in pleasing Him. That's the bottom line: you're not that interested in being golden. You're not that interested in being a Saint of Gold who is driving toward the excellence of what gold represents. Ask yourself, what does gold mean to you?

Don't discredit yourself, but know that God can still work it out for you even though you knew better and did it anyway because you thought no one saw you. Don't hang on to the guilt and shame of it. Don't feel unworthy of going after the calling you feel God has called you to do as a Saint of Gold. Don't let that hinder you from being as much of a Saint as you can be in a world that's topsy-turvy and which most people think is normal. They're buying into the normalcy of the world, but it's not normal. Things aren't normal. Things are totally different now and we can't allow ourselves to think this unbalanced and mixed-up world is normal.

Make it personal. "I know that my Father in Heaven is watching over me. He sees me and He knows me. He lives inside me and He wants me to be the best me I could possibly be even though it may take persecution, stripping me down to be that better person for others: for my family, for my friends, for the people that He puts into my life."

When I was working in downtown Seattle, I was surprised to realize there are so many homeless people on the streets in the business district. I watched the people as they walked by, totally disregarding the homeless like they weren't even there. I said, "Lord, I don't want to disregard these people, not look at them, and not notice them. I don't want to do that. I don't want to be like that, Father." That prayer was a cry for help because I know I can't do it on my own. Acknowledging someone who is homeless was the least I could do. When we, Saints of Gold, cry out for help, God is there to help us.

I really believe that the outline of this book was Divinely granted. As I'm writing this book, I'm making it personal. God in His infinite wisdom is working in our lives, individually and collectively. You may say, "I didn't grow up in a good home," or "I'm not a Christian family member..." God still has a purpose for all of that. I don't want to miss out on mine. I can't even, sometimes, believe the mere fact that I'm writing a book. I asked, "Lord, what are you doing?" but I'm excited at the same time about what He is doing. You, too, can find your purpose as you let go of the illusory inabilities and all the negative thoughts the enemy has placed in your mind to hold you back from realizing your abilities and potential. It's really an amazing thing. I'm expecting you and many others will be able to see and understand the path forward.

These days I don't listen to a lot of ministers anymore because too many of their messages have become diluted. Sadly, I think some people need to feel pain so they can begin to wake up. We've all become too comfortable, become too hypnotized by all the messages from the society we live in, and our reliance on living in the closet instead of stepping forward and proclaiming our faith as true and free Christians.

We have to wake up and sometimes it takes pain to jar someone loose from the hypnotized sleep that pervades the consciousness of many Christians.

"I know better but no one saw me."

You can no longer live your life like this!

PRAYER:

Heavenly Father, Your Power is unchanging. Your Wisdom is perfect. Create in us a clean heart and renew a right spirit in us. We confess our sins daily and Your mercies endure forever. The Saints present themselves as living sacrifices, holy and acceptable to You. Pride and humility does not mix so we humble ourselves before You for the work which is before us. We are anointed and appointed to make a difference in this world. We know better when we compromise Your Word. Forgive us, Lord. When we don't know better, help us, Lord. Help the Saints to draw nearer to You because You are our greatest Friend.

In Jesus' Name I pray.

Chapter 9

Someone's Watching Us

Someone is watching us and that "Someone" is God.

As I began to unfold in my mind and in my heart how I wanted to write about this, I did some research about the power and the magnificence of God. This led me to the beginning chapters of Genesis. We should know, as most people should, whether a Saint or a non-believer, that Genesis is the book of foundational truth for us to understand ourselves as humans and to understand the world as it has been constructed. However, research and surveys show that most people, including Saints, know very little about the Bible. They know very little about Genesis, which is the foundational truth of who we are, what we're about, our purpose, and where we are going.

We have many questions in our minds, and some of these things we don't understand, so we don't clearly know who we are as people of God, as Saints of God. My research and exploration then went on to develop my understanding of what sainthood is and what it should mean for us.

I've noticed that many believers don't take enough time to read the Word of God, to study the Word of God, and to meditate on the things of God. We should never stop reading the Word of God because the Bible, the book of the law, says so. The big question for me is, "How do we NOT stop?" We have to develop our human will and mindset to want to read, study, and meditate on the Bible because God gave the Bible to us for this reason. It's a commandment, really. It's in the Old Testament and it also, certainly, continues in the New Testament. God is watching us not only for us to have a sense of His presence, but also to see if we're looking at His Word and following the Scripture.

Secular Ideologies

We have to go back to the beginning of the Bible, to the creation of the universe and the creation of men. All these things God did in the beginning. Then, there was Satan, Lucifer, who was somehow disobedient to God. We need to go back and read and study history. You may or may not even like history! I, too, didn't like it, but because I love the Lord I now want to know the things of the past and how I became a part of this wonderful family of God. I have an interest in those things and I believe, we, the Saints, should have more interest in our history, in our inheritance instead of looking at things that really don't matter.

I know it's big now for people to go back and trace their genealogy and they even spend money for that. There's nothing wrong with this but after spending all that time, and at the end of the day does it matter more than knowing who you are in Christ? Who do you belong to? Does tracing your genealogy really matter when your life belongs to God?

I think the people who don't believe in the Bible put secular ideologies in the primary place because the world is contaminated to a great extent. The secular system put these ideologies in front of us so we can become distracted, so we can forget that God is watching us, that He's watching over us. God is watching us and He wants to perform great goodwill in our lives but we don't see that, we don't focus enough on that.

We have a system of belief that was created by God, but then a lot of people don't believe it because they have fallen off the beaten path, and the Saints have, too. The Saints have forgotten to read the book of the law, which isn't just the Torah but the book of the law that is the Bible, the complete, unerring, infallible book God gave us through inspired men who put it all together and presented it to us in words, just as I am giving this book to all of us as something we can have to advance our presence in the world, a platform of information, or a manual that points in the right direction, or whatever you want to call it.

Political System

The political system is unlawful today, and we know this because of what we see on the Internet or when we watch the news on television. We see elected men and women who are supposed to be law abiding citizens, who took an oath to help us and serve us, but then surrender to the demands of their ego and break the law. Even some Christian leaders and preachers have fallen off their thrones of grace and mercy by not doing what they preach.

Our political system exists so we can live under the authority and security of the rule of law, but the system is now corrupt and distant from the mandates of God. We, too, have strayed far from knowing that God is watching us, and only vaguely remember we're not truly of this world. Even though we want to do the right thing, we tend to be eaten by the system, by the secular ideologies, and instead we are foolishly misbehaving and ducking and dodging the behavior expected of us today as though no one is watching and, in fact, to make it worse, no one really cares.

Economic System

Baby Boomers can see a change from when we were growing up in the 50s to the system of economics we have today. Even the value of the dollar has radically changed. We used to be able to buy penny candy, big candy bars for a dime, and a dollar would go a long way. In those days we could buy some bologna, a half a gallon of milk, a loaf of bread and some candy, all for a dollar. In the same way, God was a significant influence in our society, in my childhood and probably yours, too, if you are 50 and older.

Fast forward to today, and the world promotes secular ideologies that are represented as just when they are totally unjust. As Saints we can easily be persuaded to forget that God is watching us. Are we leaning towards the ideologies of the world or are we getting back to the truth of what the Bible says about everything, including our political system? How should we be just in dealing with one another as believers, as Saints? Are we forgetting or remembering that God is truly watching us?

Educational System

As I was growing up I could remember singing Christmas songs and having a Christmas program in school. Today times have become so ungodly that we can barely mention the name of Jesus. I can say "God" but once I say "Jesus" I get a comment like, "Wait a minute, what are you saying? Did I hear 'Jesus'? No, no, Annette, we can't talk about that. God is okay, the god of the universe, but not 'Jesus'." It's okay for Easter egg hunts, too, but as soon as the mention of the 'resurrected Christ' for Easter, society wants to reject this.

The educational system has put up a truly worldly system in our schools. Now there's an opposing theory about the creation that's not Biblical. It's the theory of evolution. It was introduced in the 70s, I remember, because in my senior year the teachers began to talk about the theory of evolution in our classrooms. It's now common and acceptable to teach our children evolution, and that, Saints, is flawed, too.

We, as believers, as Saints, are forgetting that Someone is watching us. There's a God. We believe in the creation. We believe that in the beginning God created the universe, and historically it's provable. God has created everything and caused man to go and figure out the creation by creating scientific minds…the scientists, anthropologists, and all of these wonderful people who are making interesting discoveries. But these scientific minds, which God created for worshiping and honoring Him, are instead worshiping man and man's creations, and praising themselves as scientists. "Look at me, look at what I'm doing. I don't need God to tell me that this is something He's done for me; I did this. I'm the truth, I can create this. I can manifest all these things."

It's interesting how the whole understanding of who we are in God, that in the beginning God created us, and knowing that God is real and He is watching us and is for us, and that Satan is a real entity just as God is, and that Satan is representing this world, is forgotten. We're not understanding that or maybe we're not wanting to understand and believe that because of the secular world in which we live today.

The Way of Truth

The way of truth is the way. What is truth? Well, the Bible is truth. People are seeking truth and the message of the Bible gives us truth. We're seeking truth now more than we've ever sought truth before. We seek the truth of life and the understanding of life, and we seek the truth of the universe.

The truth is that the Bible has already brought the Truth to us through the Word of God. God is watching us and developing that truth because He's omnipresent, sovereign, omniscient, and omnipotent. But again, it goes back to your believing that. Do you really believe that the message of the Bible is true? Do you believe the message of the cross of Jesus is true? The Bible says you shall know the truth and it shall set you free. But what if I don't want to know the truth? Will I stumble across the truth? Will I believe that God is truly sovereign and that He's watching over the whole universe and all the people in it by accident? It's very important what you believe. Do you believe that?

Then let's go a step further. Let's say I already have that truth and I believe in this, but there's another step I have to take to understand it fully. The message of the Cross is truth and that's where our hope lies. We have the Bible, and then there's a message within that Bible which goes beyond our minimal abilities of understanding. The message of the Cross which gives us the hope, another hope beyond this world, beyond the system: God is not only watching us but dwelling with us, literally dwelling within us.

Sound Doctrines

We need to have a sound doctrine that reminds Christians that Someone is watching over us. This doctrine should direct people back to the Bible to remember and study the knowledge and wisdom that has been gathered and made available to us for our benefit.

Atheism is rampant; evolution is rampant; materialism is rampant; polytheism is rampant; and pantheism is rampant. All these things are part of our system today and a lot of people, including some of the believers who say they are Saints, are flowing with different opinions and beliefs. They're leaning toward these different -isms.

The theory of evolution is a huge -ism. Certainly, it's an important theory for scientific minds and others who are trying to minimize the fact that there was a creation. I believe the Saints are trying to compromise with the truth of the Big Bang theory to help non-believers hold on to the concept of physical evolution, but you either stand for the truth or you stand for a lie or a watered-down truth, which is also a lie.

We need a sound doctrine. Presently there are several doctrines, and we have to know and understand which are sound, and we also have to regularly read the book of the law that God gave us so we could develop our understanding. Remember, it's not just the Torah but all 66 books of the Bible that we have to study and meditate on, day in and day out. Then, we have to obey it.

The ignorance of not understanding and not believing that God is the Creator of the universe; not understanding that He is watching us and the vast universe that He created for us, caused me to think, "Lord, it is amazing what you have done for us!"

The universe is amazing. I've read somewhere that it's so vast it takes a beam of light, which travels about 700 million miles per hour, over 100,000 years just to extend across the distance of our Milky Way galaxy. Imagine an orange and a grain of sand representing the Sun and the Earth. The grain of sand is the Earth and it circles the orange, which is the Sun, at a distance of thirty feet.

In this example, Alpha Centauri, the nearest star to our own, is 1,300 miles away from the Sun. If the Sun was hollow, 1,300,000 Earths could fit inside. When you start reading and studying and getting a more complete knowledge of what God has created, and who He is, and that He truly is watching over us, it is incredible. God is watching over us and making sure we are safe and secure in this impermanent home, in this temporary home He created for us.

To me, and possibly to you, it doesn't make sense why we, the Saints, would be captivated by the secularism of today instead of the magnificence of God's creation. Why am I so captivated by this world? I don't want to be a prisoner of it anymore!

I was speaking with a friend and from the tone of his voice, I could tell I had become "too spiritual" or "too Christian" for his liking. It was sad but I also understood that although he's a Christian, he still has a yearning, a desire, to hang on to the things of this world.

He asked me, "Annette, what do you think about Christians shacking up?"

I replied, "It might be okay if planning marriage, but that's not what I do. The world does that and there's nothing wrong with it for them, but it shouldn't have a place in the life of a saint."

I asked another recently retired friend, "What do you do during the day?"

"I've been working out," she said. "I do it for a couple of hours at least four times a week now."

I added, "What else do you do?"

She said, "Me and my friends play golf but I'm still learning how to do that."

Then, I asked, "Well, what do you do to build yourself up in the things of God?"

That's when she got quiet, maybe slightly offended, or probably convicted if honest about the conversation, and then she said, "Some people can do that, Sister Annette, but that's not what I do. My friends and I hang out but I don't try to say anything like that to them. I just try to let my light shine."

I said, "Your light is shining, but maybe it isn't shining as brightly as it should. The next thing you know, your friend is dead without knowing Jesus. You didn't introduce Christ to her or say anything about Christ."

Then, she said, "That's you, Sister. I'm going to let you go now."

"I hope I didn't offend you," I said. "Know that I love you. 'Bye."

When I'm around believers, my brothers and sisters, my good words start automatically. I don't want to offend my family members. I've been polishing my gold, and the more I do, the more God wants to use it to address the trials and rewards we are going through as believers, as Saints; to address the things we are not saying to one another, the things that might even be troubling us but we're feeling too insecure to talk about. We are our brother's keeper; we are to inspire one another to a higher calling, to a better Saint, to be a genuine ambassador of truth for God.

Sound doctrine is important. I guess we are ignorant to the fact that what we already have in Christ is gold because we've been buying counterfeit for so long. We don't know that it's real gold because we think it didn't cost that much. We say, "How can it be real and not cost that much? It must not be real because it's so inexpensive."

Christ dying on the Cross? That wasn't an inexpensive deal. What He did was very costly, but why am I ignorant to that fact? Why am I ignorant to these sound doctrines; to the history of all of what God did in the beginning; to the fact that He is watching over us; the history of mankind and the Earth; the study of the dispersion of man, Noah and his descendants, from the account of the flood? That's all part of who we are.

I mentioned genealogy earlier in passing. Does knowing my ancestors really matter? Maybe people are interested in knowing they have kings and princesses in their lineage, or maybe in receiving material inheritance from their great grandfathers which was passed on in the family line. I don't know. That hasn't happened with me. Is it that important, though? Is this secular ideology more important than the biblical ideologies and the truth of God?

Mind Games

It starts in the mind and when it comes to my own mind, I know this, that I hear voices. They are not very loud or audible, in fact, but I hear them. I hear the turning on and off of the negative and the positive messages; the outlooks of pessimism and the outlooks of optimism.

When you begin to study some of these things, we just go back to the beginning where there was a fall and there was Satan. It is, however, too hard and too immense to really understand. It's incomprehensible, really. I don't understand it but I simply surrender to it.

I understand somewhat how the mind works and how it will think this information doesn't make sense. How can Someone be watching over me and watching over everyone in the whole world all at the same time? It really doesn't make sense. I could have the mindset of non-belief that there's a God who created everything. I certainly understand how people can be playing these mind games with themselves and with one another. The question is, are we, as Saints, playing mind games with ourselves and each other? Or are we being brothers and sisters to one another and behaving to one another as we should as Saints?

It goes back to that process of gold transformation, of rocks being transformed into gold. Is the heat hot enough? Am I not turning up the burner on high to heat up and make the water boiling hot, or am I leaving the water lukewarm? Am I eyeing the gold medal or am I satisfied with the bronze? If I'm trying to get the gold I may as well try and get the gold! If you end up getting the silver or the bronze, that's great, but you were eyeing the gold. So, that's what I'm aiming for with all of my being!

Have we decided to follow the world system: the political, economic, and educational systems of thought and behavior just for the sake of being a part of a corrupted secular society, or am I following these things in order to make a difference within the secular society, to make an impact for a God's kingdom here on Earth? Which choice have I made?

So, the mind game for the believers, the Saints, is the choice between selecting the freedom in which we can choose to be either/or, to lie and cheat, or be truthful and honest with great integrity and have love for one another, and not just within the family dynamic but also outside with our larger intended family of those non-believers looking on.

Common Sense or Nonsense?

He's watching over us. Well, it should be common sense but I hear a lot of times that for other people it is nonsense.

As mentioned briefly about the educational system, the hierarchy of gaining knowledge for acquiring more education like master's degrees or PhDs, is worthy. Knowledge is a great thing, especially if wisdom can be gained from it. But there is a danger in acquiring knowledge when we lose our common sense and trap or fool ourselves into deceiving ourselves that all of the great knowledge we can have in a secular system and society is good and can be used for good without including our belief in God. Can all of this education and training help me have discipline, perseverance, and conviction to create a better and more godly world?

This is all about you and I, about all of us believing in a God we can't see. He's an invisible God and yet we believe He put forth a plan and a purpose in our lives we can fulfill. Which purpose? The great commission, which is to work in a positive way to help people see the light of truth; to understand that Someone is watching us and watching over us.

Imitate God, Imitate Me

If I'm trying to imitate God, then I want people to imitate me. My family and friends know I love God. They know I talk about Him. They know I want to give myself fuel and food by reading and meditating on the Words of God. I don't wish to be and am not trying to be offensive, but I appear that I am when others don't feel like they're measuring up to me. I want the people God has divinely put in our lives to think about how they measure up. We, the Saints, need to be gold. We need to lead by example and help others aspire to wanting to be gold, too.

During the golden years when people are retired and lying on the beach, going golfing, or doing nothing, they're done. I see it too often but not with my mom and dad. They are great examples of revving up during their golden years. Then, the Lord took them Home. My dad lived a few more years than my mom, but before the "coming home" they were always on fire; they were always imitating God and saying, "Imitate me. Look at what I'm trying to do with my family." As kids, we were pretty good until we made our own choices as we became adults. Then, we made a lot of bad choices, wrong choices. We had those secular ideologies that are around us as influences. We have to remember that Someone is watching us. There may be some differences in behavior and actions but if we are taught at an early age, if we are taught while growing up, it will stick with us, and the road to return is sometimes less difficult.

We don't want our educational system to be one without Christian teachers and professors. The people that are in the educational system should be willing to say, "I will lay my life down. I will give it over. I will sacrifice my job for the sake of..." There will be sacrifices and you may lose your job or you may be called on the carpet several times. I don't know how sacrifices will work for you but I would say you must trust God and go further, knowing that He's watching us, He's watching you, and He's watching me.

God the Father, God the Son, God the Holy Spirit. Why this faith? Why this belief system? I say because it has been proven over the course of time. It has been proven that this Bible, this book that we read...or sometimes sits on our shelves...has a message that's universal. I don't know if there's another book that has that kind of effect, saying, "Wake up! Know what I'm doing, understand who you are, and be bold!" I don't know if there's another book that has helped us have the kind of influence that's historically scientific and prophetically accurate.

God is watching us as He watched over and performed His handiwork over the world at the beginning of time. We're talking about Genesis.

> "In the beginning God created the heaven and the earth. And the earth was without form, and void; and darkness was upon the face of the deep. And the Spirit of God moved upon the face of the waters." Genesis 1.

Many people may not even know that. I may ask several people to give me a Bible verse and they'll never say that one verse that's easiest to remember, "In the beginning, God..." It's unbelievable, and not only did I say that the Bible is universally influential, historically scientific, and prophetically accurate, it also has a personal life transforming power!

When you read it, when you believe it, when you understand it, then with all of the things that are happening in our world today like the Las Vegas shooting, the hurricanes, and the 9/11 tragedy, you will still believe that God is watching over our nation for a big purpose, which is to help people see the light of Christ. His nation, this nation, was born, developed, and cultivated in the biblical foundations of the truth of the Word of God. So again I ask why are we still acting casually and cavalierly knowing this foundational truth?

Wake up! Wake up, not only in the United States but in the whole world! Wake up, nations of the world! I have read the Bible and it continues to transform me. Therefore I truly believe it is true, and God is watching over us.

Relative Truth

As I was in college, I heard the term "relative truth" a lot throughout the four years I was in Pacific Lutheran University (PLU). We say truth is relative because we are afraid to stand up for the truth of the Bible. We have a lot of Christian universities that have sold out to secularism.

For whatever reasons, a Christian who is strong in the Word of God, the ways of the truth, the sound doctrines, yet remains ignorant. You heard the truth but you really haven't taken a firm stand on the truths because you haven't seriously studied the book of the law, or you haven't really desired to understand it enough, finding it too confusing, or maybe you haven't found the right version of the Bible that best helps you understand it. My advice is that you should simply get started. Tell yourself, "I am expecting more out of me because God is expecting more from me."

Difficult Times Lie Ahead

Why do I say that? Because the Bible said this in Genesis. When you begin to seek, you receive understanding and knowledge. Seek because He said, "Ask and it will be given to you; seek and you will find; knock and the door will be opened to you." Matthew 7:7.

Anyone can see today how the materialism of this secular world is insatiable. Those people who have lots of money also have huge appetites for more. After getting a fancy car and a fancy house, they want a fancy jet and a fancy yacht, then maybe two or three more of those until everything is totally bananas and over the top. These are selfish and prideful gains that go beyond having material abundance. These are self-serving egotistical and prideful acquisitions. Yes, that generosity might present itself well for those in need, but at what cost to gain it all and lose your soul for an eternity?

From the beginning, God made all these things and put them into place but now this hunger for more is unjust and ungodly. My question for you is, "How much of this are you a part of?" Are you a part of the unlawfulness; the unjustness; or the ungodliness of this system that we are in today? Again, I say, Wake up! Wake up! Wake up, Saints of Gold!"

Difficult times are ahead because our economic system is completely flawed, entirely unjust, and abysmally unlawful. Do you realize this? We forget about the truth of Someone watching us and over us, and we're supposed to be watching and helping one another get further ahead. It's up to us to get better or worse. Either we're going to learn or we're going to lose the gifts we have been blessed to receive. Let us be the Saints who are striving for the gold!

Repent and Turn Around

I say repent and turn around. Of course, it is not just me saying to repent. It can be an easy thing to do. To repent is to say, "I'm sorry. I don't want to be this way. I don't want to be a part of this," and then you turn around. You stop doing the things you know you shouldn't do. You then ask for help to keep yourself away from the influences that affect you. Know that God is watching over us and know that we need one another to build one another up; to strengthen one another; to make one another whole.

The world became so wicked and full of deceit and evil in Noah's day, just like today, and we're at a tilting point. The peoples' heart is far from God. I'm not surprised but I am sad. It's very sad to see that the believers, the Saints, can have a lot going on right in their own families and never address this at all in the spiritual sense. The Saints don't let people know that God is watching; that Someone is watching over us; and that there is a real God; and the Bible is true.

Saints need to speak up and ask their family members simple questions like, "Have you accepted Christ as your Lord and Savior? Does He have any impact in your life?" That's a great thing! Our duty as men and women of God is to fear God and to keep His commandments. Knowing and doing our duty begins when we're really young, but if you didn't get to learn and know this when you were young, the super-natural process only starts to happen when you surrender your natural man and stop saying, "I am a god. I know my own destiny." Stop believing the lie; the world continues to perpetuate. God knows His own; let go and let God.

God has innately put it in us to know there is something we can't quite figure out. When we start understanding the truth that God is truly watching us and over us can we surrender to Him and repent, and turn around. Meditate on the book of the law every day and you will succeed. That's what the Bible says. It's not the worldly success, however. Think beyond this world. Think "…on Earth as it is in Heaven." We think about the things beyond this world because that's where we're headed, to the next world. The question you must answer is "Do you believe?"

Not only do you believe, but do you believe strongly enough to make your actions reflect your belief? We can believe all we want but if we don't take action and provide evidence of our belief in practice in our lives, our belief is shallow because it hasn't been given power through our actions. That's when we see the real Saints of Gold. We'll see who is gold and who is silver and who is bronze and who is copper or tin…

It takes a lot of concentration to consistently be authentic as a Saint of Gold. It most assuredly is intentional in all ways. You can't let down your guard. You have to be constantly on point. The one moment you're not steady, fingers will point at you and the non-believers will shake their heads and say, "I told you so."

There are many who watch us so they can feed their own cynicism, but we are accountable only to ourselves and to the Sovereign God to whom we pledge our eternal faith.

PRAYER:

> *Heavenly Father, You alone are worthy of Praise. Heaven is Your throne and the earth is your footstool. Do we believe that You are watching everything? Help our unbelief, Lord. Saints can overcome temptations, we can influence others, we can do all things through God who strengthens us. We are the salt and the light. We do not hide behind closed doors because You are the Door. We will no longer walk in the darkness as though no one is watching. We hear Your voice because we listen. You are All-Powerful and All-Knowing and see everything we do. Where can we go to escape from Your Spirit, Lord? Nowhere. You see in the dark and the daylight because they are the same to You. Help us to not forget the benefits of being Saints, striving toward perfection in this corruptible body until we become incorruptible with You forevermore.*
>
> *In Jesus' Name I pray.*

Chapter 10

The Gold Standard... What Is It?

It's important to look closely at the gold standard and come to a clear understanding about what it is and how to give it a priority and meaning in our lives.

We've looked at the gold standard from the standpoint of the Olympic Games' gold medals, and how an athlete has to dedicate all their time, all their focus, all their energy to compete successfully with other super-athletes who also want to be recognized as the best athlete in the world in their field.

Even though they are all working as hard as they possibly can, only three athletes will receive Olympic medals and for all their effort, they may never achieve even the bronze medal, but these athletes also know they have to strive for the gold if they are ever to achieve the goal they desire so much. Even if, as happens with most, athletes at this level never win any Olympic medals, they are still recognized as outstanding in their field and they take it as a solemn and hard-earned honor to compete at the national and world level.

In the same way, Saints of Gold don't quit, and we also strive every day, and every moment of every day to be the best Saint we can be, always striving to be better in our relationships with others and with our self, always improving ourselves to more completely carry and present God's Word and God's Will to those people we meet in the course of our life's path.

We've also looked at gold as a process requiring extraction from rock or gold fields where gold is hidden in the earth. The rocks are crushed or the earth is filtered to draw the valuable gold through the sluices so it can be melted in crucibles and turned into solid bars. It's an intensive process requiring hard work, but these labors result in tremendous reward.

Then there are the Golden Years, the time of life that follows the years of dedication, working and saving so you can enjoy your time in retirement. However, our work as Saints never stops, and we continue to fulfill a life of excellence, improving ourselves so we can constantly become more capable of serving God.

Truly Free

In order to be a Saint of Gold, we need to have a true understanding of the Word of God, we need to be committed to the Word of God. It doesn't take much to realize there is a lot of room for growth and improvement. Many of us say we believe in the Word of God and we are committed to it, but we truly aren't, and since this is the case, we aren't truly free.

We live in a great country, a country that espouses freedom, equality, and justice for everyone, and yet we know this is not completely realized. There are many injustices we see in the news and in our daily lives, but we do have the intention to be free and equal in the eyes of each other and the eyes of God. We live in a perfectly imperfect world, a fallen world where God is Sovereign, and each of us is here to purify ourselves for the purpose of helping one another become truly free. To be truly free means living a life according to the concepts of the Bible. True freedom is in Him, in the Word of God. No other freedom is as complete, as meaningful, as important as that freedom which is available only through our connection with God.

Conditions

There are some conditions to being free in this most complete sense, in the sense of our liberation through God's Word. I'll name just a few, and the first is believing. Believing usually starts with the foundational upbringing in our childhood when our mother and father, together with our pastor and Sunday school lessons taught us about God and Jesus, about His sacrifice for us, and taught us as children to believe.

If you didn't receive this blessing as a child, you can still go back as a teenager or adult and study the Bible and its supportive works and begin the process of becoming a dedicated Christian and Saint of Gold. The same is true if you didn't grow up in a Christian home. Eventually you will be exposed to situations that cause personal reflection, and if you are a mature thinking and feeling person, you'll examine the meaning of your life and hopefully come to a place where you acknowledge there is a compassionate and loving God, and that the universe was created by Someone. The universe was not created by accident, and even though we cannot fully understand it, this didn't just happen from some random chance of cause and effect. Someone deliberately created all that we know and all that we don't know, and made this world exist the way it does. Having belief in this basic idea is the starting condition for truly being free.

The second condition for being free is having an unyielding commitment to learning about the Word of God through the Bible and related teachings, and taking action to bring your life in alignment with Christian practices. The choice is either to commit to God's Word, which is available to us in the Bible, or merely go along with the status quo of the secular world which diminishes or eliminates the role of God and establishes man-made rules, laws, and ideologies that don't really help us live a decent, clean, healthy and wholesome life. Just look around! A person who is not committed to understanding the Word of God as it was given to humans to understand, and by extension is not committed to improving themselves according to the Word of God, is not a truly free person.

The commitment of wanting to seek and always know a little bit more, wanting to do a little bit better than before, and willing to love with more enthusiasm are all elements of the gold standard. Everyone reading this book right now is a Saint, but just in case you're not and are not convinced you are one, you can always be more open-minded, do more research, be less restrictive with how you think and behave, and allow this new way of perceiving and living to take place. Just give it a chance. Give gold a chance. Let gold do what gold does! It doesn't tarnish, lose its value and is much desired. This is how you can gain your true freedom. This is a true Saint of Gold.

Perseverance

True commitment takes perseverance, so that's another condition for attaining your true freedom. A person who perseveres will continue a defined course of action whether it is easy or whether confronted with great difficulty even when the prospect for success may be limited. When you persevere, you set your mind and behavior to complete whatever task you've selected. You've committed yourself to your goal, and whether it's a one-day goal or a one-week goal or a lifetime goal, you've chosen to complete your mission in thought and action.

In this case, you have every chance for success because we live in a great country with the right to practice whatever religious beliefs you have, provided they do not harm anybody else. In the United States we have freedoms and liberties many countries do not have, and because of this it is much easier to be a Saint of Gold here, more so than many other countries around the world. Of course, we wish to spread the freedom of God to all the people in every country that want to be truly free, and as Saints of Gold it is our responsibility to disseminate the Word of God and the truth and the true freedom it brings.

Sacrificial Living

As a Saint of Gold we will be called upon to sacrifice our time and our personal energy to serve others in the name of God. When you are called upon to do God's work, you may have to miss a round of golf, or decide to miss a show at the cinema so you can be with a friend or neighbor who needs your help. You may be called upon to do something that is an investment in somebody else's life and yet, this same investment of sacrificed time is truly an investment in your becoming a better Saint of Gold. Going outside your comfort zone, sacrificing your pleasure so you can give support and Christian guidance to someone who needs to hear and rely upon the Word of God. All of this is an act of obedience and service towards a loving God in which we certainly benefit.

You might also be called upon to sacrifice some of your material wealth. You might hear that a nearby family is struggling to put healthy food on their table, and the $100 you were planning to use in a restaurant with your spouse suddenly seems to have a better purpose. In your giving is also your opportunity to plant the seeds of your faith, to use your ministrations of love and charity to show others the way toward their true freedom.

As you know, we have a lot of fat cats here in America, and that's great. There is nothing wrong with being a fat cat…but are you selfishly keeping what you have and continually trying to get more of the American dream for yourself, or are you thinking of others as well as yourself and being mindful of the gold standard required of all Saints? How can you help others receive some of the same benefits you've received through the grace of God?

Restart and Re-Plan

Do you remember the biblical story of the Rich Young Ruler? It's in Mark 10:17-27. Jesus was on a journey and he was approached by a wealthy young man who asked Jesus how he could inherit eternal life. Jesus told him to sell all his possessions and give them to the poor, but upon hearing this, the young man became gloomy and walked away because he was unable to part with all that he owned.

Will this be your story, too? Are you so encumbered by worldly friends and influential people, so weighed down by property that it owns you instead of the other way around, and will cause you to give up the

Kingdom of Heaven for the comfort of this life instead of the glory of the next?

Saints of Gold know they can restart and re-plan their lives each and every day. We can look back to the trials of yesterday and see where we had our pitfalls, where we came up short, where we defeated ourselves because of our selfishness, our ego, our pride. With the perspective of time, we can see how certain choices led to specific situations that were either blessed or cursed and we now possess the hindsight to make better choices if we will, to make the right choices that improve our connection with God and with our ability to bring God's Word through us to the benefit of others.

When I think of my neighbor, for example, I question how I can improve that relationship. That's a restart. Then when I think about what I can actually do that improves the relationship, that's a re-plan. Perhaps I can invite him or her over to a little social gathering that I have next time, or when I see him or her out in the yard I could make a point of saying a few nice words about all the work that's made the garden look so attractive. I could also go knock on his or her door and bring some cookies I've baked. This doesn't have to be complicated; simple will do just fine.

Another nearby neighbor has some health issues, so I can make a point of going over to his or her house and asking, "Are you doing okay today? Is there anything I can do for you?" That's a restart. It doesn't take much to restart or re-plan anything. It's all in how we view what we do and not comparing what we do with what others do for us. We can choose to be the Big Sister or the Big Brother, lending a hand in helping those we see around us. We can also be the Little Sister or Little Brother and receive gifts of Spirit from like-minded Saints who see us struggling and in need.

These gifts of Spirit are the seeds from the Word of God, and they are planted in the warm soil and moisture of the souls we greet so they, the seeds and the souls, can blossom under the sun of our Lord and Savior.

As we walk our daily path, we need to consciously be aware of how we're cultivating, nurturing, grooming, pruning, and helping the seeds we're planting in our lives to restart and re-plan, and set ourselves toward our desired gold standard even as we plant the seeds in the lives of others.

Harvesting Your Crop

As we purify and sanctify ourselves by becoming better at what we do, as we improve at being Saints of Gold, we'll notice the many little things we've done that help others improve their life's plan, help them make a new start in life, assist others with moving forward while having a better outlook and purpose in life. This is the harvest we are privileged to see as others have seen the harvest in us because of the gifts they gave.

The first harvest isn't always about planting the seeds of the Bible. Rather, it's just showing love, care, and compassion. It's showing that you are a person they can count on, a person they can rely upon. The gold standard is being able to look at a person and see their need, and then fulfill that need in some way, even as simply as giving a smile. Something as simple as a smile can make a person's day; I know it's made mine many times.

Sadly, many people have not had a hug all week, so going to church is a great opportunity to show love and give someone a hug. Yes, it may be a sacrifice on your part because you may not be the hugging type, but when you obey the Voice within, which propels you to more, and you remember the Big Picture, that you are a messenger of God, that you are a Saint of Gold, you will find a way to give that hug to a person who needs to know that God loves them, that they are not alone, that they are safe and seen and loved. We have let the world become cold and cruel, but it does not have to be this way any longer. We have it in our power to be kind and compassionate and this is the greatest treasure of all, for both the giver and the receiver. Giving love does not deplete the resource, it embellishes and expands it! When you give love there is always more to give. This is another example of God's enormous grace.

Exercising Your Faith

Part of exercising our faith is extending ourselves in offering our service to others in God's Name. We should also be exercising our faith in our homes, and do this daily. Of course, if you have children living with you, exercising your faith is very important so your children can learn who they are and understand their purpose in life by witnessing you exercising your faith and living up to the gold standard.

When your children come home from school, inquisitive and asking questions, you should give those answers that matter in the long run;

answers that help them understand what they need to know for their eternal life. It's important you give them information that's biblically-based and not restricted to the limitations of the materialistic society in which we live. Do not let the establishment culture make you afraid to talk about God who has created the heaven and universe. Our corrupted culture wants Saints to ignore the truth of the Word of God. There is a God and there is a devil. Who will you believe? Whose side will you be on, Saint?

If you're on God's side, there are things you must do to claim the gold standard. You might not even know you're not yet a Saint of Gold because no one has challenged you. You might think you are a true Christian, and yet it's an eye-opener when you read about the percentages of Christians, perhaps including you, who are not behaving in the ways that exemplify a true Christian and Saint of Gold.

A recent study by the Barna Group, an organization that does spiritual and religious research, caught my attention. This study was conducted among practicing Christians in the United States to gauge how much the tenets of other key world views, including New Spirituality, secularism, postmodernism and Marxism have influenced Christian beliefs about the way the world is and how it ought to be.

Barna said they found a strong agreement with ideas unique to non-biblical world views among practicing Christians. This widespread influence upon Christians' thinking is evident not only among competing world views but even among competing religions. For example, 38% of practicing Christians, which is nearly four Christians in ten, are sympathetic to some Muslim teachings. 61% agreed with ideas rooted in New Spirituality.[1]

The number of Christians in the United States who call themselves "practicing Christians" is 75%. How many of these Christians are experienced in expressing our faith? Of these 75%, 61% agree with ideas rooted in New Spirituality. How does that make you a Gold Saint? Well, it doesn't. These Christians are at the bronze level, or maybe lower.

It gets even more interesting. 54% resonate with post-modernist views. 36% accept ideas associated with Marxism. The one that surprised me the most was that 29% accept ideas based on secularism which

---

[1] https://www.barna.com/research/state-church-2016/

embraces biological evolution! 23% of Christians strongly agree that what is right or wrong depends on what the individual believer thinks. All of this is simply amazing to me.

Barna defines "biblical world view" as believing that absolute moral truth exists. The Bible is totally accurate in all the principles it teaches. Satan is considered a real being or force, not merely symbolic. A person cannot earn their way into Heaven by trying to be good or doing good works. Jesus Christ lived a sinless life on Earth and God is the all-knowing, all-powerful Creator of the world who still rules the universe today.

Much has changed in the United States, in the last 10 years especially. We have a new law that same-sex marriages are legitimate. We continue to live in an increasingly secular humanistic American society. Americans are attending church less than ever before.

These statistics show the erosion of fundamental, biblical, and foundational truths among Christians. Many Christians no longer know or espouse the biblical foundations that are essential to living a wholesome Christian life. It's quite likely that in the next 10 - 20 years the situation will become even worse. Unless we hold up the gold standard, we could possibly see the extinction of Christian practice and belief in this nation. My point is that you need to get yourself in a quiet place without any distractions, be still, do not speak, and humble yourself to hear what the Lord has to say regarding what you're doing as well as what you're not doing. And quickly!

These types of non-Christian behaviors do not allow you to succeed in the way that's pleasing to God. It's God's will for men and women to be married, not partnered in relationships as two women or two men. To those of you who are homosexual, I'm sorry. I identify myself with God, the Creator of the universe, the One who has set the standard, and set it high. It's God's will that the adulterer stop, the fornicator stop, stop any and all emotional and or physical relationships regardless of the loneliness and love and respect that has established itself among you. We can reach the gold standard instead of the one of tin.

With these new cultural secular standards that encourage Christians to think it's acceptable to practice Christianity in undisciplined non-Christian ways, it's important you see you as a soldier participating in cultural warfare that's happening within our nation. If you are exercising your faith but you're doing it all wrong, then really, you're not doing it at all.

Here are more statistics on church attendance in the United States. It's good that 75% of all Christians in the United States consider themselves practicing Christians. It would be far better if 100% of all Christians exercised their faith on a daily basis, but that's a discussion for later.

According to Barna, 20% of Americans claim no faith at all, so these are the atheists, the people who are grounded in the secular world and are not interested at all in anything spiritual. Of the 75% practicing Christians, 55% actually go to church. If we break this down, that means that of all the Christians in the United States, only about 40% attend church regularly, which seems rather dismal. 34% actually read their Bible. Only 19% volunteer at a non-profit organization, which might be their own church.

I can verify the last statistic because I saw how few members of the congregation at my church volunteered for various projects and events. What about the other folks that ain't doin' nuthin'? "Oh, I'm burned out! I'm already wearing two hats! I'm just too tired!" This one always gets me: "I'm waiting on the Lord to tell me what I should do." Really?

17% attend adult Sunday school, and 16% attend small group instruction. These numbers are staggering to me! I'm glad I go to church, and I'm glad I'm in the participating portion, and I'm improving in every aspect of my dedication and devotion to serving God, and so must you.

I want you to improve in every aspect, but how will you know you are improving? When we're around each other, gold will magnify itself with gold. If I can see you have something in silver and I want to help you get gold, I'm going to encourage you and help you improve, and I will never tire of extending the gold within me that I want to share with you. This is the way Christians can help each other, can help all of us strengthen the foundation of our belief and faith, and help us rise to the gold standard of true freedom as Christians.

That's what this is, extending my love as God extends His love. Exercising my faith, and exercising your faith, becomes a daily commitment requiring daily perseverance. Eventually this grows and becomes a lifetime commitment with lifetime perseverance.

This is how our life goes on until we die, but that gold standard never tarnishes or diminishes, and never goes away. When your time has come to be in Heaven, you've left a great legacy, a great treasure of gold that has enriched the lives of others and made a powerful difference in this world.

Seek understanding in everything because God's hand is connected to everything. Follow your inclinations and let God lead you where He will as you study the Bible, as you spread the Word, as you proclaim the good news. Learn to be open to new information and new relationships. Seek unity through love and compassion and helping one another. Develop a spirit of excellence founded on truth and look to resolve conflict between people whose hearts are good though they may have different opinions.

Get Understanding

As you study and learn and experience the path the Saints of Gold tread, eventually you will be blessed with understanding and wisdom. You can't get it yourself because these blessings are God-given. When we understand that there is a God who knows all, sees all, and who is sovereign, we won't get bogged down trying to understand what can't be understood.

What we can understand and what we have is the gold standard as a set of spiritual behavior expectations. This concept was established thousands of years ago, and it's the truth and wisdom we need to embrace so we can become better people on this journey of life.

Lift Up Your Voice

Now is the time to lift up your voice. Be brave and speak out. Have faith in your God-given strength and say what you know and what you believe. Tell the truth and let people know you have an answer to their questions; you have divine facts to present against the culture's fiction. Let people know you're not prideful, but you have a message that's worth gold and you want your voice heard because God is speaking through you.

People can be humble and loving and generous, knowing what they know is the truth, God's truth. I applaud people who speak up and have a true sense and understanding of what God has done for them. Whether you are rich or poor, we all have the ability to obtain the gold standard and live our faith as true and free Christians.

Fed Up, 'Fess Up

So…are you fed up? Are you fed up because of the way our nation is, because of the way Mr. Smith is, or Mrs. Green is? Are you fed up because of how your teacher is, or perhaps how your child is? Lots of people are fed up with the way things are today. The truth is there's a lot to complain and be fed up about. Family dynamics are breaking down, people around us are less polite and more rude, common courtesies are antiquated, the media is constantly bombarding us with negative news and instructions to buy more, and the world itself has become a more dangerous place to live. Yes, many of us are fed up. Many of us have had enough. Many of us are ready to throw in the towel!

If that's the way you really feel, then you also need to 'fess up…'fess up to the truth, 'fess up about your weaknesses. 'Fess up about your inabilities and your insecurities, 'fess up about your fears. 'Fess up about all the attitudes and behaviors that prevent you from becoming the best Saint you can be. If you are fed up, then 'fess up!

By 'fessing up a Saint can come along and help you get back on the path, can help you dig out the gold-bearing rock that lies within you and help you bring forth the Christian qualities that will set you free.

Today nearly half of the United States is unchurched. Half of the United States, and 75% of that half say they identify with Christians and Christianity, but I wonder how they identify with Christians when they don't go to church.

The secular world has its perspective, and I have mine. The secular world can speak its mind and proclaim what it wishes, and so can I. I'm going to say what I wish to say as you, World, are saying what you wish to say, so don't hate me, secularists. Don't call me a bigot and label me homophobic and all of the other things you say when I'm trying to reach out to you in love.

That's not the way we do things! We are Saints of Gold. I didn't come up with that name…that's the name God gave me to use so I could talk about the diminished standards of Christian life and behavior, and encourage Christians to step forward and step up, to profess their belief in God and Christ without fear, to say we love God, we believe in Christ, and we can say and do these things with love.

I hope we can construct and create something better than what we have now, and that we can create this new way of living our faith through love, but not the love that people think is love. It goes beyond that. It goes beyond the post-modernism definition of what love is. It's deeper than that, it's so deep that once you get this deep inside yourself and seek it out, there'll be an awakening in you, and you will come out a totally transformed person. This isn't about your intelligence, having a PhD, or being a CEO or seminary scholar or professor, though of course we are all appreciative of your intellect. Thank you!

Personally, I'm finding this process is very transformational for me. Many people in our society have become quite skeptical and cynical with institutionalized religion because it has broken its trust with people and doesn't seem capable of activating God in our lives or having Christ in our hearts.

What we need is for people to stop pretending they are Christians and truly become Christians, and for Christians to truly behave like the Christians Jesus wanted us to be. We need people, Christians, Saints of Gold who are actively involved with others, actively involved with other Christians and non-Christians and who exemplify the love and compassion that Christ showed everyone He met.

Clearly we can't all be as pure and capable as Jesus, but each one of us knows there is always more they can do personally to help others they see and meet in their daily life, and there is more each of us can do to develop our knowledge and abilities as Christians, and with spreading the good news. If we continue to remain silent about our beliefs in God and Jesus, then we are blocking the Word of God from reaching the ears and lives of people that need to know, that are in great pain and will benefit by seeing our example and bringing God's love and grace into their lives.

Our Christian practices and the service we give to one another truly matters. The experience of being a true Christian is transformational, and when we choose to be a Saint of Gold, each one of us will find that our life changes for the better, transforming ourselves as we bring transformational change to others.

That's what this book is about. It's about helping people realize, helping YOU realize, the only real answer is within. When you tap into the power that exists through your belief and your faith, everything is possible and nothing can resist the change that's available to every one of us.

I'm excited for us! When you think about your life and where you've been, and about where you've come from and see all the little steps you took to get here, it's exciting! You will find there is no contentment more satisfying than living your life as a true and free Christian, speaking about your faith to those you see, and sharing your faith with other Saints of Gold who strive daily to build and strengthen the community of the Saints of Gold. Then you will find yourself in a Heaven on Earth while journeying toward the 'New Heaven and New Earth.'

It always comes down to a matter of attitude. How a man or woman thinks, that's how things are. When you think you can't succeed, when you think no one loves you or cares about you, when you believe you're ugly or stupid or shameful and no one will talk with you or accept you, these are only representations of the active enemy within.

You are greater than that. You are much, much more than this. You are the beloved child of a loving God who is asking you to live your life in a Christian way that creates love and understanding in the hearts of people who are hungry to know true peace and freedom.

I hope you accept this challenge and become a Saint of Gold. You will be blessed and feel great joy in your heart by truly being who you are. I know you will find the loving sanctuary of peace and freedom you have been seeking.

May God always abundantly bless you!

PRAYER:

> *Father in Heaven, You are the Ruler of this world. You are the Father of all life. You are the Creator of all men, but Father to those only who know You and keep Your commandments. We Saints have been chosen before the foundation of the world and remain here today for such a time as this. We, the army of God, will not retreat, we will not stop lifting up the name of Jesus, we will not be afraid, because we are equipped to do Your plan, which is to go and make disciples, baptizing all in the name of the Father, Son and the Holy Ghost.*
>
> *In Jesus' Name I pray.*
>
> AMEN

Made in the USA
San Bernardino, CA
15 June 2018